JOSEPH MARIA
OLBRICH

JOSEPH MARIA OLBRICH

IAN LATHAM

RIZZOLI
NEW YORK

Front cover
Haus Olbrich, watercolour perspective, 1900.

Half-title
Haus Olbrich, master bedroom, watercolour
perspective, 1900.

Frontispiece
Grosses Glückert Haus, south elevation.

First published in the United States of America in 1980 by

Rizzoli INTERNATIONAL PUBLICATIONS, INC.
712 Fifth Avenue/New York 10019

Library of Congress Catalog Card Number: 79-64341
ISBN: 0-8478-0230-2

Printed and bound in Great Britain

CONTENTS

Foreword   7

1. EARLY WORK AND THE VIENNA SECESSION
Early Years   9
Vienna Secession   13
Ver Sacrum   15
1st Secession Exhibition   17
'The Golden Cabbage': The Secession Building   18
Vienna Projects   34
Café Niedermeyer   40
Villa Friedmann   42
Haus Bahr   46

2. DARMSTADT ARTISTS' COLONY
Establishment of the Colony   48
'Ein Dokument Deutscher Kunst'   50
Ernst Ludwig Haus   52
Haus Olbrich   58
Haus Christiansen   68
Grosses Glückert Haus   70
Kleines Glückert Haus   78
Haus Habich   84
Haus Keller   86
Haus Deiters   90
Provisional 1901 Exhibition Buildings   92
1904 Artists' Colony Exhibition   98
The Wedding Tower and Exhibition Buildings   100
Opel Worker's House   112
Oberhessisches Haus   116
Glückert Haus Redecorations   118

3. OTHER WORK IN GERMANY
Miscellaneous Projects 1899-1908   120
Low Cost Housing Projects   138
Haus Silber   141
Warenhaus Tietz   143
Last Days   147

List of Buildings and Projects   149
Bibliography   151
Plan of the Mathildenhöhe, Darmstadt   152
Acknowledgements   154
Index   155

FOREWORD

If the reputations of individual designers rested solely on their creative genius and diligence, then Joseph Maria Olbrich would undoubtedly have been considered long ago alongside the great masters of the early twentieth century. This, however, has not been the case; to date there has not been a detailed study of the architect's work available in any language. The vast majority of references, both written and illustrative, are contemporary. Hermann Bahr, Ludwig Hevesi and Joseph August Lux were among Olbrich's acquaintances to provide valuable early documentation and it is fortunate that drawings and photographs of his work were carefully collected and presented in *Ideen,* his 'Ideas', (1900, 1904), and in a large portfolio published by Ernst Wasmuth of Berlin (1901-1914).

In more recent years research on Olbrich has been undertaken by Robert Judson Clark, Othmar Birkner, Gerhard Bott and Karl Heinz Schreyl, the latter being responsible for the compilation of a comprehensive catalogue of the 'Olbrich Sammlung' in Berlin Kunstbibliothek where the vast majority of the architect's drawings are collected.

This study is the eventual result of a chance visit to the site of the Darmstadt Artists' Colony in the summer of 1976 as a third year architectural student seeking a suitable thesis topic, and I am deeply indebted to the many individuals who have provided advice and assistance between then and now. Thanks are firstly due to many students and staff at Oxford Polytechnic's Department of Architecture, past and present, notably Reginald Cave, Timothy Hodson, Paul Oliver and Tom Porter for their early encouragement and guidance. The illustrative material for the book has been gathered from various sources with the help of Dr. Marianne Fischer of the Berlin Kunstbibliothek, H. J. Painitz, President of the Vienna Secession, and Dr. Rainer Schoch of the Hessisches Landesmuseum in Darmstadt, in addition to staff at the libraries of the Victoria and Albert Museum and the Royal Institute of British Architects in London. Stuart Durant and Dr. Andreas Papadakis were kind enough to lend further material from their collections. For the purpose of clarity I have redrawn many of the line illustrations included in the book, keeping as close to the originals as was possible; a note to this effect is included in all of the relevant captions.

Finally I would like to express my gratitude to Frank Russell, Vicky Wilson and Richard Kelly at Academy Editions for their patience and expertise and to all family and friends who have endured my enthusiasm.

Ian Latham
London 1979

Grosses Glückert Haus, lamp in the entrance portal.

'The modern applied artist must be a poet and a practitioner at the same time, then he is creative and exuberant for new things. Then he can combine arts and crafts in special and compelling ways. Then he is original, an individual personality, because the first discovery that the creative individual instinctively makes is simply: he himself. The artistic personality is his own being. In this book Olbrich is just such an applied artist.' (Ludwig Hevesi, Introduction, *Ideen von Olbrich,* Wien, 1900.)

EARLY WORK AND THE VIENNA SECESSION

EARLY YEARS

'Nothing human seems to be strange to this artist. For in everything he is himself. What he creates is not English, Belgian or Japanese, but "Olbrichisch". An intimate communication from the artist, a self-confession.' (Ludwig Hevesi, Introduction, *Ideen von Olbrich,* Wien, 1900.)

Joseph Maria Philipp Olbrich's creative talents were, it is said, first brought to notice at the work-table of his father. The eldest son of a baker, Edmund Olbrich, and Aloisia (née Neisser) Olbrich, Joseph decided not to enter the family business with his two younger brothers. He did not settle happily with the academic pursuits at the Staatsgymnasium, and resolved to follow his passionate interest in architecture, going off to learn building construction.

Born on December 22nd 1867 at 15 Ratiborerstrasse in Troppau, the capital of the Austrian Duchy of Silesia (now Opava, Czechoslovakia), Joseph Olbrich left school before taking his final examinations, the Abitur. After working briefly for the Troppau building contractor Hubert Kment, he departed for Vienna in September 1882 at the age of fourteen to enroll at the Staatsgewerbeschule in the building department under Julius Deininger. In the following year Camillo Sitte was appointed as Director of the School. A town-planner and architect specially interested in urban structure, Sitte was one of the first important influences on the young Olbrich's development; they also shared an enthusiasm for the music of Richard Wagner. Joseph Olbrich returned to his home town of Troppau in the summer of 1886 to work for the contractors firm of August Bartel. Here he was employed as a designer and job supervisor and, it appears, attracted the attention of Bartel himself whose enthusiasm and encouragement persuaded Olbrich to return to Vienna. The earliest surviving drawings by Olbrich date from this period; his scheme for a house and restaurant building in Belgrade for a Dr G. Dimitrijewic illustrates well his competent drawing technique.

In October 1890 Olbrich enrolled at the Special School for Architecture at the Academy of Fine Arts in Vienna (Spezialschule für Architektur, Akademie der Schönen Künste) under the leadership of Baron Carl von Hasenauer. Together with Ferstel, Hansen and Schmidt, Hasenauer had been responsible for the Ringstrasse project — the great road lined with monumental buildings, built on the site of Vienna's 'glacis', the ramparts that had enclosed the old city. These architects 'were artists of large ideas, but themselves imposed limitations on their capabilities, in the belief that only in one or other of the historical styles could they give expression to their architectural aims. They enjoyed a great reputation in Vienna, and settled for years to come the direction of architectural activity there. But while their surpassing talent enabled them to thoroughly master the ancient styles without sacrificing their independence, their pupils and imitators, on the other hand, became hopelessly enslaved to these styles. With them all that an architect need do was to copy, with more or less skill but without a particle of "geist", the examples given in the text-books.' (Hugo Haberfeld, 'The Architectural Revival in Austria', *The Studio Special Number* 1906, cii.)

Olbrich's talents flourished at the Academy. In his first year he was awarded the Füger Medal and the Pein Prize, and he won the second prize of 200 florins in the competition for the Silesian Museum of Fine Art in Troppau which he entered in addition to his school projects. The Drexler brothers were placed first in the competition, for which the judges included Hasenauer and Bartel. In the second year Olbrich received a prize for his project for a Ruhmeshalle (Pantheon), closely resembling the works of Hasenauer, who awarded his favourite pupil the 'Special School Prize for Architecture'. To the envy of his fellow students it seemed a mere formality when in the third year Olbrich was announced as winner of the Rome Prize — 1,500 Gulden for study in the Eternal City.

In the Academy Exhibition of July 1893 Olbrich displayed his final school project, a scheme for a monumental theatre. It was here that the promising young student first came into contact with Otto Wagner. 'At the annual visit I make to the school exhibition of the Academy, out of curiosity and to ascertain the level of achievement, was added the fact that in 1893 I was also seeking assistants to help with the execution of the architectural aspects of the Stadtbahn. Under Hasenauer, Olbrich had prepared a theatre project for the school exhibition (still completely traditional and pure Hasenauer), but this project surpassed all the others at the time in its graphic skill. I enquired about this student and learned that he was in the building. I met him in the vestibule, and straight away he happily accepted my offer of employment.' (Otto Wagner, 'Josef Olbrich', *Die Zeit,* August 14th, 1908, p.1.) Otto Wagner was not in fact given the Stadtbahn project until 1894.

Olbrich worked in Wagner's office for the few months until November 1893, during which time he completed a series of large competition perspectives for Wagner's Vienna development plan. He then left Vienna and headed southwards to take up the Rome Prize, stopping in Bolzano and Padua before journeying on to Rome itself. There, in contrast to the usual procedure for prize-winners, Olbrich did not set up a studio and, after four winter months, left the city. In a letter to Josef Hoffmann, his friend and colleague at the Academy, and later recipient of the Rome Prize, Olbrich revealed: 'Everything bad and good of great and ancient renown has an odd effect on a sensitive mind. The bad seems to lead a victorious struggle against the good and had I not brought so much enthusiasm and piety from home with me, that too would perhaps have seemed bad . . . Rome teaches well what is great and mighty, but what seems to be of most importance for our age — I have not even found here in embryo.' (K. Moser, 'Unbekannter Brief Josef Olbrichs: römische Eindrücke' *Neues Wiener Journal,* November 7th, 1931.)

During March and April of 1894 Olbrich travelled further south, his dated sketches of landscapes, seascapes and traditional dwellings indicating the route: Naples, Sorrento, Capri, Amalfi, Paestum, Salerno, Pompei and Benevento. He then crossed to Segesta on Sicily where he received a letter from Otto Wagner pleading for him to return to Vienna to assist with the increasing work load of the Stadtbahn, the project for the extension of Vienna's suburban railway network. Olbrich nevertheless continued on to Tunis where he terminated his trip in May of 1894. Otto Wagner personally asked for the remainder of the Rome Prize to be held in abeyance, whilst Olbrich returned to his office to take up the appointment of Chief Draughtsman for the Stadtbahn project.

The exact extent of Olbrich's architectural responsibility for the Stadtbahn buildings remains unclear. It seem likely, however, that in addition to the detailing of many of the stations he designed the exteriors of the Hofpavillon at Schönbrunn *(Ver Sacrum* of August 1899 attributes it to Olbrich, Carl Fischl and Leopold Bauer, and this is confirmed by Ludwig Aloys who worked on the interiors) and the station on the Karlsplatz with its distinctive sunflower frieze. Usually Otto Wagner would sketch a design in outline before passing it on to Olbrich for completion; Olbrich occasionally concealed his signature somewhere on his drawings. Following the death of Hasenauer in 1894, Wagner had been appointed to lead the Academy School of Architecture, so a great deal of responsibility was put on his young assistant's shoulders; Olbrich even began to

Olbrich's last student project at the Vienna Akademie for a theatre, shown at the Akademie Summer Exhibition of 1893.

Sketch of a grave at Posilipo made in spring 1894.

share Wagner's own private office. Meanwhile Josef Hoffmann had joined the office staff. Otto Wagner treated his talented students as if they were his own children; he was apparently very disappointed with the architectural abilities of his own son. Olbrich was a frequent visitor to Wagner's villa at Hütteldorf for Sunday lunch, and Wagner was later to contemplate the marriage of his two daughters Louise and Christine to Olbrich and Hoffmann.

There is reason to believe that the master-pupil relationship between Wagner and Olbrich was not entirely in one direction. Wagner can be considered as one of the true founders of the Modern Movement, calling for the replacement of the irrelevant plagiarism of historical styles by a new architecture based on 'purpose' and employing 'appropriate' materials. Wagner's own buildings, however, never completely broke away from the classical framework; this task was to be accomplished by his students. Nevertheless, Wagner's later buildings, such as his Post Office Savings Bank, Steinhof Church and other contemporary projects owe much of their originality and inventiveness to the inspiring enthusiasm of the younger generation of Viennese designers in the so-called Wagner School.

In March of 1895 Olbrich again left Wagner's office to resume his Rome Prize travels, but this time he headed westwards and visited Germany, France and England. Few details are known of his trip and only a small number of drawings remain.

Otto Wagner: Linke Wienzeile 38, 1898.

On his return to Wagner's office Olbrich began, with Wagner's approval, to undertake various projects in his own time. These included a competition entry for the Reichenberg Museum. No prizes were awarded as so many of the entrants had exceeded the stipulated budget, but Olbrich's and Friedrich Ohmann's drawings were purchased for 300 Kronen each. An altered version of Ohmann's design was later built. In 1896 Olbrich received a 600 Gulden second prize in a competition for Laibach Assembly Hall, and in the same year, together with the engineer Eduard Swoboda, he produced an unsuccessful competition entry for the replacement of the Franzensbrücke (Francis Bridge) in Vienna.

In 1898 Wagner was commissioned to produce a scheme for the new quarters of the Academy of Fine Arts. Olbrich was heavily involved in the project and was credited with the design of the central Hall of Honour. His inventive skills flourished within the limits of Wagner's underlying classical framework. The monumental Hall had a fundamental formal quality, yet Olbrich's fantasies broke through in clusters of wreath-bearing maidens, wrought-iron serpents and a metalwork laurel halo. Although the project was never actually built it aroused a great deal of attention when shown at a Secession exhibition.

Otto Wagner: Karlsplatz station, 1898.

Otto Wagner: station at Schönbrunn, 1896.

VIENNA SECESSION

In the second half of the nineteenth century, Vienna had, to a greater extent than almost every other European city, undergone extensive replanning in a whole range of neo-classical styles. This was highlighted particularly by the Ringstrasse project, the broad road and band of buildings erected on the site of the old city walls. Hermann Bahr relates: 'The styles of yesterday no longer please; those palaces, decorated like ones from the Renaissance or from the Baroque are no longer effective. We demand to live in the ways that match our requirements, just as we dress in the ways that match our requirements. We don't want costumes any more, neither do our houses. If we go over to the Ring we find ourselves in a right cheap carnival. Everything is hidden, everything is disguised, everything is masked. But life has become just too serious for that. We want to look life in the face. We use the catchphrase of a "realistic architecture". By this we mean that the building should serve its purpose, it should not conceal it but express it distinctly. Whoever has the strength to give constructive solutions to his forms is our artist. To hide them behind strange forms seems foolish and ugly to us. Previously one would first demand that a building should "look like something". We demand that it should be something. We are ashamed when present day working people live like the princes or partricians of yesterday and the day before yesterday. We feel that's a swindle. From the building one should see what it is, what is the profession of whoever lives in it and how he lives. We are not Baroque people, we don't live in the Renaissance, why should we act as if we did? Life has changed, fashions have changed, every thought, every feeling and the whole art of the people has changed, so the people's buildings must change, to express their new tastes and deeds. Such wishes have been loudly voiced and will no longer be silenced.' (Hermann Bahr, *Secession*, 1900, p.109.)

The visual arts in Vienna were dominated at the time by the Academy of Fine Arts and the Künstlerhaus. These two conservative establishments exerted an effective stranglehold on the artistic life of the capital, the former as the respected training ground for Vienna's artists and the latter as a private association owning the city's only permanent art exhibition building. The Künstlerhaus, under the leadership of the architect August Siccard von Siccardsburg, was therefore free to influence Vienna's cultural life through a careful selection procedure for its exhibitions.

In December of 1894 Julius Deininger, Karl Seidl and Otto Wagner supported Olbrich's application for membership of the Künstlerhaus which, with the endorsement of three such prominent architects, was readily accepted. The Künstlerhaus exhibition of the same month was uncharacteristically liberal in content and proved a great success for the younger Viennese artists. There was little room in existing Viennese circles for those artists who wished to question, discuss and seek beyond the confines of the established theories. So from 1895 a number of the younger artists would meet in the 'Zum blauen Freihaus' for a meal whilst others gathered for coffee at the 'Café Sperl', often to examine the latest copy of *The Studio* magazine from England. This group called themselves the 'Siebener klub' (Club of Seven), and included Joseph Urban, Max Kurzweil, Leo Kainradl, Adolf Karpellus, Koloman Moser and the architects Josef Hoffmann and Joseph Olbrich. The latter two were often joined by their employer Otto Wagner, by now in his mid-fifties.

Dissatisfactions with the narrow-minded approach of the Künstlerhaus increased through 1896 and were strongly voiced by Gustav Klimt, Carl Moll and Josef Engelhart. The final catalyst occured in November 1896 when the conservative Eugen Felix was re-elected as President of the Künstlerhaus. Bearing in mind the approaching golden jubilee of Franz Joseph I, he initiated measures planned to exclude many of the more radical members from exhibiting at the Künstlerhaus and more especially from its shows abroad. The ageing painter Gustav Klimt emerged as leader of the dissidents. They demanded an autonomous association along the lines of the breakaway group in Munich, and formed the 'Vereinigung bildener Künstler Wiens- Secession' — the Vienna Secession. Gustav Klimt was elected as their President.

The Secessionists intended to remain in the Künstlerhaus, but on May 22nd 1897, soon after they had made preliminary enquiries for an alternative exhibition building, the Künstlerhaus administration passed a motion of censure on the members. Klimt and Olbrich walked out of the meeting and on May 24th thirteen signatories submitted their joint resignations. These included the nine original Secession members — Gustav Klimt, Ernst Stöhr, Johann Viktor Krämer, Koloman Moser, Carl Moll, Rudolf Bacher, Julius Mayreder, Joseph Olbrich and Josef Hoffmann. The group was soon joined by the respected painter Rudolf von Alt (1812-1905), who became their Honorary President, and later, in 1899, by Otto Wagner. Honorary members listed in the first issue of the Secession magazine included Walter Crane, Eugène Grasset, Max Klinger, Max Liebermann, Auguste Rodin, Franz Stuck and Fritz von Uhde, and by the second issue they were joined by Edward Burne-Jones, F. Knopff and E. A. Walton. Alphonse Mucha had been an ordinary member from 1898. 'In Munich and Paris the intention of the Secessions has been to replace the "old" art with a "new" art . . . No, with us it is different. We are not fighting for and against the traditions, we simply don't have any.' *(Ver Sacrum* No. 1, January 1898, p.9.)

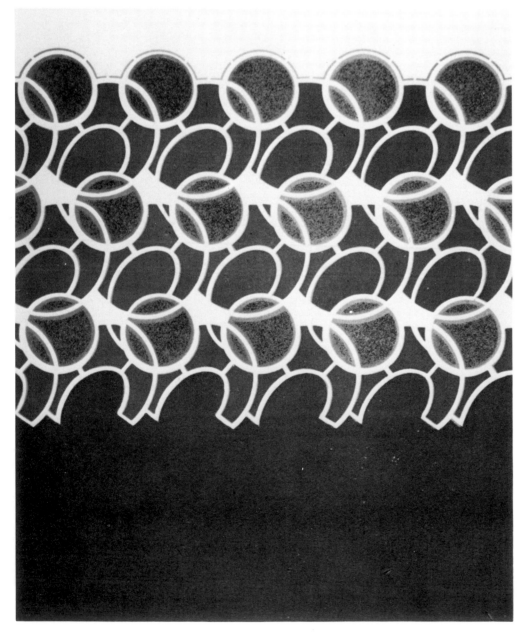

Decorative frieze designed for the Villa Friedmann, 1898.

VER SACRUM

The first move undertaken by the Secessionists was to set out and announce their intentions. At the First General Meeting on June 21st 1897 a decision was taken to publish a magazine to achieve this. It was to be called *Ver Sacrum,* meaning 'Sacred Spring' or 'Offerings of Firstlings'. This would introduce the Secession's aims and provide an effective show-case for their own work and the work of foreign artists, long ignored in the traditional artistic circles of the capital.

The initial issue of *Ver Sacrum* (January 1898) announced: 'NOW EVERY AGE HAS ITS OWN SENSITIVITY. It is our aim to awaken, to encourage and to disseminate the art sensitivity OF OUR AGE, it is the main reason why we are publishing a magazine. And to everyone who is striving for the same goals, even if by a different path, we gladly extend a hand for alliance.'

'We want an art not subservient to foreigners, but also without fear of foreigners and without hatred of foreigners. The art from abroad will encourage us to reflect upon ourselves; we shall acknowledge it, and admire if it deserves it; only we will not imitate it. We want to bring foreign art to Vienna, not just for artists, scholars and collectors, but in order to educate the great majority of artistically receptive people, so that the latent instinct that lies in every human breast for the beauty and freedom of thoughts and feelings will be woken.'

'And then we turn to all of you, without discrimination of status or means. We recognise no distinction between "high art" and "minor arts", between art for the rich and art for the poor. Art is public property.'

'And so one of you says: "But what do I need an artist for? I don't like pictures", then we will answer him: "If you don't like pictures, then we will decorate your walls with delightful hangings; perhaps you like to drink your wine from an artistically designed glass: come to us, we know the shape of the vessel that is worthy of the noble drink. Or do you want an exquisite piece of jewellery or an unusual fabric to adorn your wife or your sweetheart? Speak, try it just once, and then we shall show you that you can get to know a new world, that you can conceive and possess things, the beauty of which you have never dreamed, whose sweetness you have never tasted!" ' *(Ver Sacrum* No. 1, January, 1898, p.6.)

Sketches for a garden wall and entrance to a state prison featured in *Ver Sacrum,* 1898.

Bearing a close resemblance to *The Studio,* the influential English arts magazine that had opened the eyes of the Siebener-klub members, *Ver Sacrum* provided the ideal vehicle for the development of graphic ideas and techniques by the artists, notably Moser, Olbrich, Hoffmann and Böhm. It was on the pages of *Ver Sacrum* that Art Nouveau made its first appearance in Austria, arriving later and to be abandoned earlier than in most other countries. Olbrich and Hoffmann developed their characteristic ornamental styles in the magazine, the former employing circles and combinations of circles, the latter using more rectangular themes, but both owing a debt to contemporary English graphic work, the 'geometrical-symbolism' of the Glasgow Four and some aspects of Gustav Klimt's paintings.

Imaginary drawings, c.1898: 'Architectural sketch' and 'The gods live on cloudy heights'.

1ˢᵗ SECESSION EXHIBITION

Much of the initial year of the Secession's existence was devoted to preparations for their first exhibition. Negotiations for a site for a permanent Secession headquarters ran into difficulties, so it was decided to hold the first exhibition in an existing building. The premises of the Gartenbaugesellschaft (Horticultural Society) on the Parkring were hired for a three month period, for a considerably higher rent than would normally be charged to more reputable organisations. Olbrich and Hoffmann were given the task of the arrangement and display of the exhibition.

Hermann Bahr, art critic and supporter of the Secession, tells of his first meeting with Olbrich: 'You won't remember any more, dear Olbrich, how we got to know one another. At the time you were arranging the building of the Gartenbaugesellschaft for the first exhibition of the "Vereinigung"; I came along a few days before the opening. It was that wonderful time in March, when it's still bleak and cold, but you nevertheless believe that you can already feel spring in the air . . . In just such a mild fever I would rather run on and on to the end of the world than enter that dull place with its sawing, nailing and hammering and everyone hurrying about almost despairing that it would ever be ready. In the middle of this confusion and bustle of shouting and moaning people I caught sight of you standing, with hat on head and an elegant cane, or rather a light rod, that you were effortlessly twirling in your hand, appearing rather as if you were at a masked ball, seeking adventure. To every question you had an answer, to every request a word of advice, for every complaint a consolation, cheerfully giving out your instructions in the best of humour. When someone said it would have to be postponed, you said: "It will open on time!" When someone despaired, you said: "But everything will be ready!" When someone panicked, you said "Don't get excited, children!" You nevertheless had such a calm and confident mockery in your cheerful eyes that the people really believed you and were pacified and again took heart. I however thought to myself in wonder: "Look, there for once is a real man; he'll be alright." And so we shook hands and chatted for a while, and then I took my leave, while you stood calmly in the hall, twirling your cane.'

'Since then we have met occasionally and each time I have again thought: "A man who is capable of anything!" ' (Hermann Bahr, *Secession,* Wien, 1900, 'V. Meister Olbrich. In Froher Bewunderung'.)

The 1st Secession Exhibition was the earliest commission executed by Olbrich under his own name. He designed the entrance and main exhibition rooms, whilst Hoffmann was responsible for the administrative office and the temporary office for the magazine. The works were hung at eye-level and arranged in their respective groups, contrasting in both respects with the traditional ways of the Künstlerhaus. Careful consideration was given to the backgrounds, using matt white, dark red and dark green canvas to harmonise with the pictures without distracting from them. The decorations included a stencilled frieze of long-stemmed flowers in dull gold, though this was not considered to be particularly successful.

The exhibition was opened on time, and ran from March 26th to June 15th, 1898. Besides works by the Viennese members of the Secession, many foreign contributions were shown, including some from Rodin, Whistler, Mucha, Knopff and Crane. Walter Crane, the first English honorary member of the Secession and familiar to Vienna's artists through his regular contributions to *The Studio,* sent watercolours, drawings, book illustrations, wallpaper and stained-glass for display. The 1st Secession Exhibition proved to be not only an outstanding public success, with Franz Joseph among the early visitors, but also an economic success; many of the works were sold, providing a substantial financial basis for the construction of a new exhibition building.

Gustav Klimt: poster for the 1st Secession Exhibition held at the Vienna Horticultural Society Headquarters, 1898.

17

THE GOLDEN CABBAGE: THE SECESSION BUILDING

'Olbrich is a man highly gifted, impulsive and imaginative, a poetic interpreter of space, and a decorator of rare taste. Through Wagner he acquired self-restraint and a severely critical attitude towards himself and art. Still Olbrich retained so great a fund of enthusiasm that he became the leader of the younger generation of architects. His Vienna buildings, true documents of "Ver Sacrum", have all of them provoked the fiercest conflict of opinion. His first effort was the "Secession" building, erected during the space of a few months, a work vigorous and fresh in conception, sober yet impressive, well-proportioned and graceful, and withal a personal creation yet dictated by 'purpose'. The particular problems presented by an exhibition building have never been better solved; the interior has been so planned that instead of being fixed the walls are movable, so that any desired portion of the space may be available with top light or side light.' (Hugo Haberfeld, 'The Architectural Revival in Austria', *The Studio Special Number* 1906.)

The Secession first approached the Innenministerium (Interior Ministry) to request a site for a temporary exhibition building in February 1897. The sympathetic administration offered them a prominent piece of land on the corner of the Wollzeile, facing the Ringstrasse, which belonged to the War Ministry and had previously been used for temporary art exhibitions. Although some early sketches for a design were made by Gustav Klimt (dated spring 1897), and the early Secession members included the architects Josef Hoffmann and Julius Mayreder, it seems to have been generally accepted from the beginning that Joseph Olbrich was to be given responsibility for the design of the Secession building.

'With what joy did I give birth to this building! It arose from a chaos of ideas, an enigmatic clue of the lines of feeling, a confusion of good and bad; not easy! There were to be walls, white and shining, sacred and chaste. Solemn dignity should pervade. A pure dignity that overcame and shook me as I stood alone before the unfinished temple at Segesta. There I conceived the germ of that contempt with which I face clumsy pieces of work that are concerned with everything but with warmth, with the heart. And when I understood the task with the heart, when the inner feeling grew louder than mind and spirit, then I also had the fortitude to produce what I felt; and it was born!'

'So it was that I found the forms that seemed to truly embody my feelings, and that said to me that they expressed what I wanted to say and indicate. I wanted to invent neither a "new style" nor "Modern" nor even the "latest"; that would be an accursedly vain undertaking! No, I wanted to hear only the echo of my own sentiments, to see my warm feelings frozen in cold walls. Subjectivity, my beauty, my building, as I had dreamed, I wanted and had to see. The task was put before me and, as usual with subjectively inclined artists, no limitations were put on my creation. It was now my noble right to show my idea of beauty, to say that it has to be done with the heart, and that everything measured with the proportions of traditions and the traditional aesthetic teachers appears foolish and awkward. A full heart gave me this courage, strong individual feelings, my own beauty.'

'That's how the building came about. It grew up in six months, hand in hand with the construction; today the form has frozen, and I see in reality what appeared to be good expressive means. Today I would design some things differently, let it freeze with more feeling; but everyone knows best what the problem is.' (J. M. Olbrich, 'Das Haus der Secession', *Der Architekt* V, 1899, p.5.)

Secession Building, entrance facade on the Friedrichstrasse; the inscription reads 'To Every Age its Art. To Art its Freedom'.

WOHNHAVS · D^R · HERRN · D^R · STOHR

Preliminary sketch of the Secession building on the Wollzeile site, 1897.

Opposite above
Stöhr house and shop, St. Pölten, 1899, watercolour and chalk perspective and tinted elevation.

Opposite below left
Secession Building, sketch for the preliminary scheme on the Wollzeile site, 1897.

Opposite below right
Café Niedermeyer, sketch for the first floor salon, 1898.

By the end of March 1897 Olbrich submitted his initial design. Sharing a familial resemblance with Otto Wagner's Stadtbahn buildings, and still bearing the mark of Olbrich's Baroque education, the fluent perspective sketch for the temporary building shows elements of the final scheme, particularly in respect of its symmetrical facade with a central entrance flanked by an arrangement of blocks and towers. Doubts about the suitability of the design were voiced, particularly concerning the axis, and Olbrich was also asked to change the facade; he submitted detailed drawings in September, which move closer towards the final solution. A stylistic debate ensued, and opposition mounted from the War Ministry who were concerned with the visually disturbing effect of such an alien building on the prominent site, and the consequential detrimental effect on the value of adjacent property; negotiations came to a standstill. Severe criticism had come from various councillors backed up by a number of newspaper reporters. The Secession, nevertheless, was not without influential supporters, including the Mayor of Vienna, Karl Lueger, and councillor Rudolf Mayreder (brother of Julius, the Secession member), who were aware of the valuable contribution that an independent association of artists could provide to the cultural life of the

21

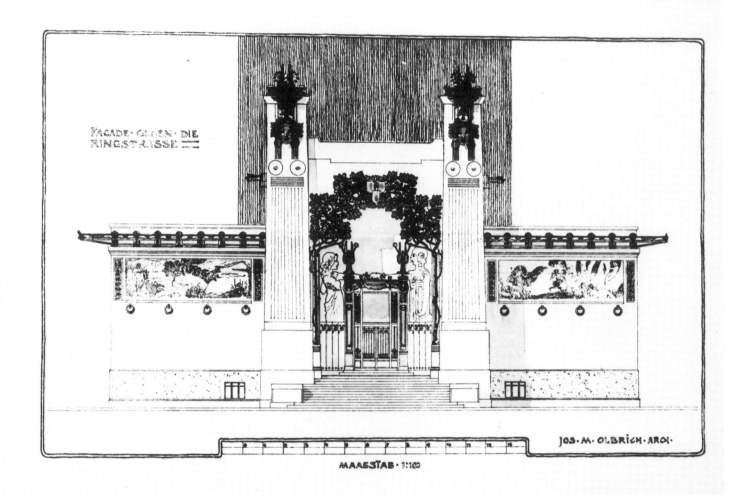

AUSSTELLUNGS - GEBÄUDE
DER VEREINIGUNG BILDENDER KÜNSTLER OESTERREICHS.

FACADE · GEGEN · DIE
RINGSTRASSE

JOS · M · OLBRICH · ARCH·

MAASSTAB · 1:100

First scheme for the Secession Building on
the Wollzeile site: *(above)* perspective,
(opposite) entrance elevation, *(right)* sections.

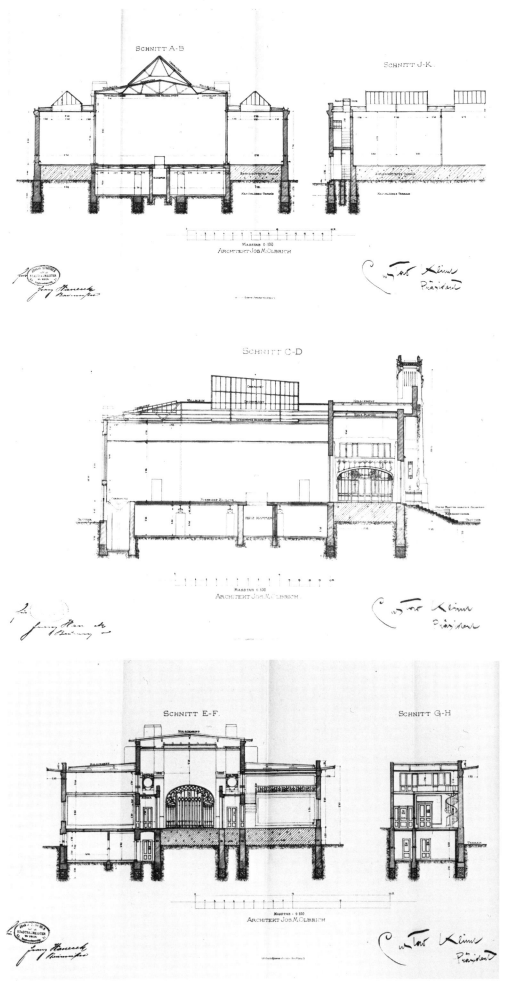

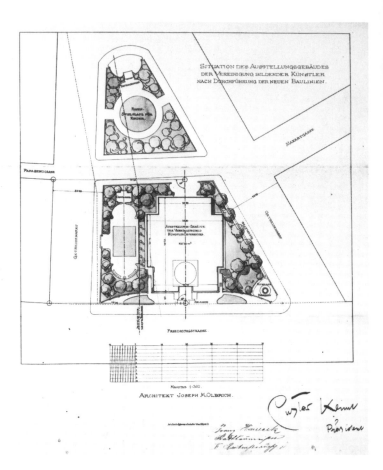

Second scheme for the Secession Building on the Friedrichstrasse: *(left to right)* perspective, site plan, ground floor and basement plans.

capital, and who did not wish to interfere with their artistic intentions by imposing restrictions on the form of their exhibition building.

So in October 1897 when Carl Moll, the forthright Vice-President of the Secession, suggested a new site for the building on the Friedrichstrasse, approval was quickly granted (17.11.1897), and the responsibility for the artistic form of the building was left in the hands of the architect.

Olbrich set about producing a scheme for this alternative site, for the first time introducing the idiosyncratic dome. He completed the drawings, working on them in his spare time from Wagner's office, and submitted them in mid-March 1898. Approval was granted on April 6th and the foundation stone was laid on April 28th. The construction was financed by the profits from the 1st Exhibition, for which the artists had given their services free, and through donations from the wealthy Mautner and Wittgenstein families.

'If at the present time you go down by the river Wien in the early morning you can see there, every day behind the Akademie, going from the town to the theatre, a throng of people crowding round a new building. There are workers, craftsmen and women who should be on their way to work, but they stop here, staring in amazement, unable to turn away. They gape, they question, they discuss this thing. They think it's extraordinary, they've never seen anything like it; it disturbs them, they are really taken aback. Serious and lost in thought, they go on their way, turning around again, having another look back, not wanting to leave, and hesitating to hurry off to work. And that just doesn't stop the whole day long.'

'The building is the new Secession building, by the young architect Olbrich. It should be handed over to the city on the 4th of November: on the same day the first exhibition will begin inside it. I believe there will then be a great howling, the senseless people will be enraged. I would therefore rather say now what is necessary. Now it can still be done quietly and impassively, later there will be a scramble.'

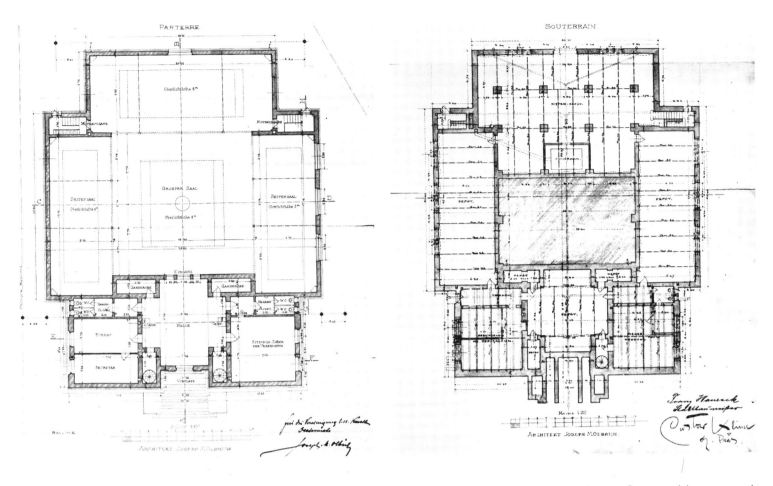

'Let's go inside. First we enter a room that seems solemn. One could compare it with a Propylaeum. It is thought of thus: as a vestibule in which those entering shall feel cleansed from everyday cares and put aside the worries or moods of the common world, and prepare themselves for thought, like as it were a quiet seclusion of the soul.'

'Then we enter the building. Here everything is dictated by function alone. Here there was no attempt to please in a frivolous way, to show off or to dazzle. This is no temple or palace, but a space which will allow works of art to be shown to their greatest possible effect. The artist has not asked himself: how do I make it so that it looks best? but: how do I make it so that it best fulfils its functions, the needs of the new tasks, our demands? Here facts alone have determined everything; what the circumstances require was the only rule. It has been created as one would create a fine wheel: with the same precision that thinks only of purpose, with no thought of prettiness, but seeking the true beauty in the purest expression of the requirements. The requirements: the standards of lighting, soundness against stormy weather or snow, the security of individual works are fulfilled here with unsurpassed wisdom, and it hasn't been forgotten that our art will be otherwise unimpeded; it has been anticipated that more and more, as the artists express it, the "Pictorial art" will be superceded by the "Interior art"; it has been foreseen that it will be necessary to be able to change the work, like with a spell, at a stroke and to be able to adapt again to each new challenge.' (Hermann Bahr, *Die Zeit*, October 15th, 1898, p.42. Also in *Secession*, 'Meister Olbrich', p.60.)

Still today the Secession building retains its bold simplicity and it is not difficult to imagine why its radical form caused such a storm at the end of last century. The central doorway is flanked by two blocks and surmounted by four piers supporting a gilded dome of laurel leaves. The exterior is finished in white painted stucco, which led Hevesi to suggest similarities with the work of C. F. A. Voysey (see Ludwig Hevesi, 'Das Haus der Secession', *Fremdenblatt*, 11.11.1898). The extent to which decoration was intended on the exterior of the building is uncertain; some early sketches indicate that the blind facades at the front were to

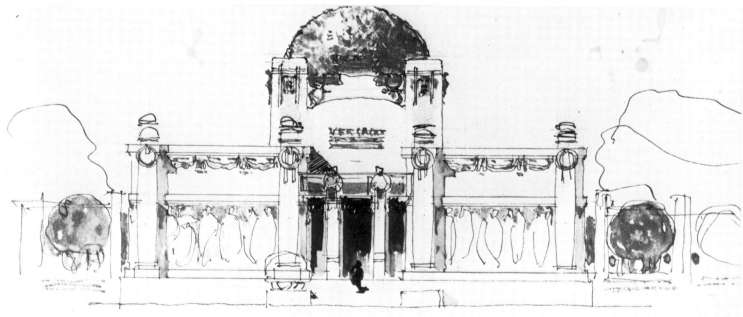

be filled with murals, although Olbrich's final drawings leave them clear. The decorative embellishments that were carried out serve to complement the Secession building without distracting from its essential simplicity; these originally included twisting stalks leading up to a lush frieze at the entrance, a group of Minerva's owls, drawn by Moser and modelled by Olbrich, and a frieze of dancing girls on the rear elevation by Koloman Moser. The entrance provides a strongly symbolic image, as does the gilded dome which echoes that of the Karlskirche across the square. Dark red marble steps, flanked by laurel bushes (real, in contrast to the dome) approach the bronze doors by Georg Klimt, younger brother of Gustav. (The existing doors are replicas made by Rudolf Kedl in 1965.) The masks and snakes above the doorway were sculpted by Othmar Schimkowitz.

Entrance elevation (from the original drawing) and preliminary sketch for the Friedrichstrasse scheme.

Opposite
Entrance facade on the Friedrichstrasse and detail of the gilded dome of laurel leaves.

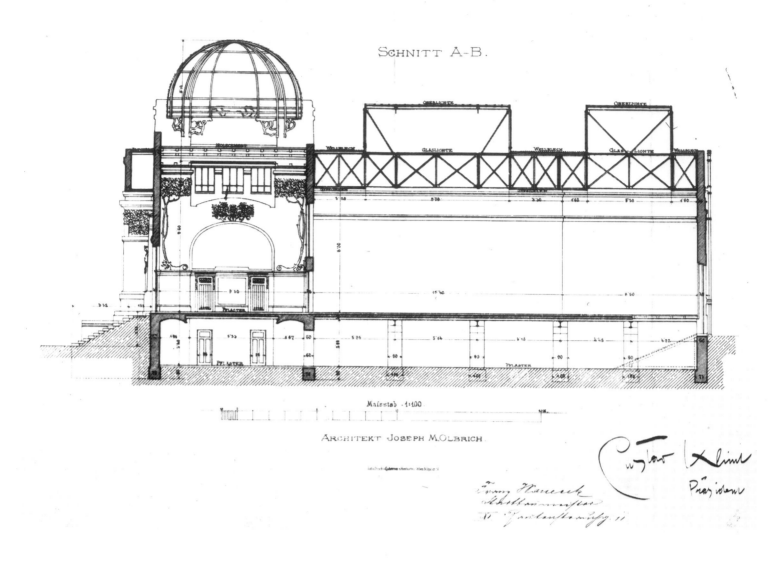

SCHNITT A-B.

Maßstab · 1:100.

ARCHITEKT JOSEPH M.OLBRICH.

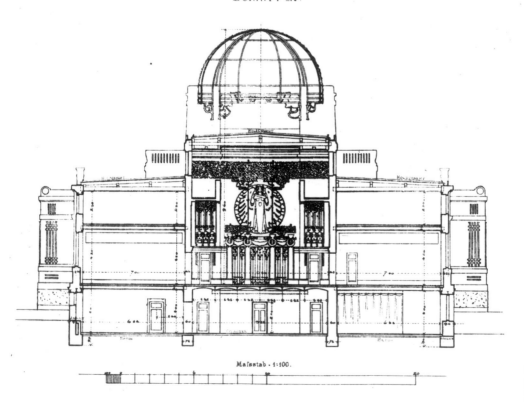

SCHNITT EF.

Maßstab · 1:100.

Olbrich's final drawings for the Secession
Building on the Friedrichstrasse site:
longitudinal and lateral sections.

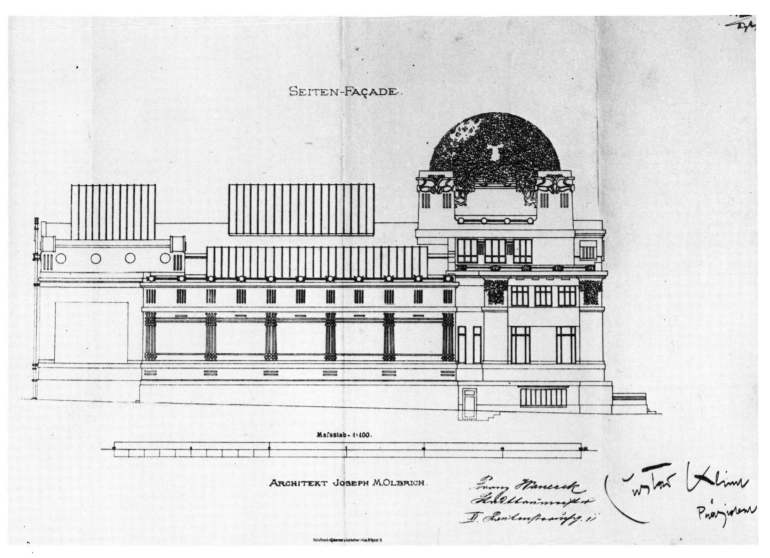

SEITEN-FAÇADE.

Maſsstab - 1:100.

ARCHITEKT JOSEPH M.OLBRICH.

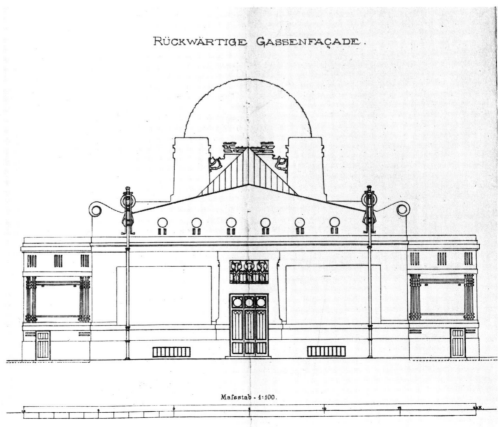

RÜCKWÄRTIGE GASSENFAÇADE.

Maſsstab - 1:100.

Final drawings of the side and rear elevations
of the Secession Building. The original
drawings bear the authorising signature of the
Secession President, Gustav Klimt.

'Function was the substantial influence on the arrangement of this building: to provide by the simplest means a useable structure for the activities of a modern artists' association. It was therefore made spacious, correctly dimensioned in width and height, with exhibition rooms lying on one and the same level, arranged for ease of orientation on a main axis, a heating and ventilation system designed to achieve equable, comfortable temperature conditions, and a lighting-system arranged so that all parts of the exhibition rooms receive the same even, steady light and to avoid the appearance of reflections on the hung pictures.'

'In order to adapt the room parts of the exhibition halls for the individual exhibitions and to be able to achieve as varied an overall view as possible, the roof of the building was placed on six supports, whilst the partitions located between them can be adjusted over the whole area of the rooms.'

'For exhibitions of interior design, rooms are provided with side lighting. Moreover the building contains a reception room in the hall, in addition to the rooms required for the administration and a conference room, then in the basement is service accommodation and the necessary depots and packing rooms which are linked with the street as well as the exhibition halls by variable ramps, and finally the premises necessary for the editing and control of this journal. The exterior form of the building is crystallised from all these requirements, and itself seeks to emphasise the solemn dignified definition of the building as a home of art. The white and gold formulated architecture is worked out in its overall form as well as in detail in relation to the existing large site area in front of the building. The exhibition building, that has already passed its test at the 1st Exhibition with excellence, is in design and execution the work of the Vereinigung member, architect Josef M. Olbrich.' ('Das Haus der Secession', *Ver Sacrum* 1, 1899, pp.6-7.)

The Secession building became a popular target of ridicule. Carl Schreider described it as 'a little Egyptian, some Assyrian and a little Indian, no wonder therefore that on the whole it appears "Spanish" to the great majority of people'. (Carl Schreider, *Deutsches Volksblatt*, November 19th, 1898). This is perhaps not surprising as Olbrich was undoubtedly influenced by the vernacular dwellings of the Mediterranean area that he had seen on his travels. Hevesi heard the building called 'a cross between a glasshouse and a blast-furnace' and an

Present condition of the Secession Building: *(opposite)* view from the Friedrichstrasse and rear elevation, *(above)* details of the stucco decoration; the owls were modelled from a design by Koloman Moser.

'Assyrian convenience', and later it became known more affectionately as the 'Golden Cabbage'. (Ludwig Hevesi, 'Das Haus der Secession', *Fremdenblatt,* November 11th, 1898.)

Just over six months after the foundation stone had been laid, the Secession building was opened for the 2nd Secession Exhibition on November 12th 1898, its total construction having cost only 60,000 Gulden. The exhibition included drawings and plaster models of Otto Wagner's scheme for the new Academy of Fine Arts, for which Olbrich was named as a chief assistant. Unusually, a whole room was devoted to the applied arts and included works by William Morris and Walter Crane as well as wallpapers by Olbrich and Hoffmann. The central exhibit was a large sculpture by Artur Strasser of the Mark Antony group, which was later modelled in bronze for showing at the 1900 Paris Exhibition. (Today it stands outside the Secession building.)

'Half a year ago everyone just laughed at the new Secession building. Today it is already the pride of the Viennese. I fear that in another half year it will be a model for the eager copiers to build churches, hotels and villas: in ''Secession Style''. What a change in a few years! What a change in the artists' intentions! What a change in the wishes of the public!' (Hermann Bahr, *Secession,* p.111.)

'The word ''Secession'' caught fire; everything outré bore the title ''secessionistisch'', and as in painting and architecture there were true and false Klimts and Otto Wagners, so in the arts and crafts there were true and false secessionists. But what a world lay between the two! The stranger coming to Vienna, who knew nothing of Josef Hoffmann, Olbrich, Koloman Moser, Plečnik, Leopold Bauer, Jan Kotĕra, Adolf Böhm, Roller, Krauss, and other secessionists in the arts and crafts, must have shrunk from ''Secession'' with a feeling of horror that in a city famous for art such ''un-art'' should be found, and

Entrance with sculpture by Othmar Schimkowitz, present and original condition.

longed for those bronzes, leather goods, porcelain and other objets d'art for which this historic city had long been celebrated. ''Secession'' has survived this, for it is no longer a by-word, but one to which all honour is due. Even the split has made little difference in this respect. The ''Secession'' has done most to bring about the modern development in the arts and crafts; it showed what other nations were doing, and introduced, among others, the Belgian, English and Scotch schools to Vienna.' (A. S. Levetus, 'Modern Decorative Art in Austria', *The Studio Special Number* 1906.)

Olbrich's poster for the 2nd Secession Exhibition, 1898, the first to be held in the new headquarters.

Right
Interior views of the 4th Secession Exhibition, 1899.

Below
Present site of Artur Strasser's sculpture.

VIENNA PROJECTS

Following the first two Secession exhibitions and the completion of their building, Olbrich's architectural and design talents were recognised. Commissions resulted which he carried out whilst remaining in Otto Wagner's office, with his employer's complete approval. The majority of these were for interior schemes and furniture for wealthy friends and supporters of the Secession together with a number of private houses. Olbrich continued to work in Wagner's office for a total period of five years until the summer of 1899, by which time he was receiving enough commissions to set up an office in his own right, albeit somewhat briefly. His address of Hechtengasse 1 (now Rienosslgasse) had also been the administrative address of the Secession before the opening of their own building.

One of Olbrich's earliest commissions still in existence was the Bicycle Clubhouse built in 1898 for the Vienna State and Court Officials' Club. The simple structure cost 10,000 Gulden and was erected during the construction of the Secession building. It is now used as a clubhouse by a tennis club on Rustenschacherallee 7. The building is contemporary with a grave Olbrich designed for Isodor von Klarwill, editor of the *Fremdenblatt,* who died on May 8th 1898; this remains in good condition in the Döblinger cemetery. On the granite base was a figure by Artur Kaan and a verse by Ludwig von Doczi, whilst four bronze serpents supported a small bush, providing an interesting allusion to the Secession dome.

Drawings exist for various minor projects carried out by Olbrich during 1898, including a Staatsgefängnis (state prison), sketches for graves, and a scheme for the Jubilee Memorial Church of Franz Joseph for a competition won by Viktor Luntz.

In 1899 Olbrich designed his first complete house for Dr Hermann Stöhr, brother of the painter Ernst Stöhr, in St. Pölten. (The house, at Kremsergasse 41, is still in existence.) Sited on a main street between two existing buildings, the ground floor contained three shop units whilst Dr Stöhr's residence and premises were on the two upper floors. Careful consideration was given to the fenestration: three deeply recessed arched windows were arranged on the projecting first floor and a wide window was placed off-centre on the second floor, balanced by a mural of a female figure holding a bowl, and an Aesculapian snake executed by Ernst Stöhr.

Olbrich modernised the interiors of Alfred Stifft's house on the fashionable Hohe Warte. The Vienna wine merchant was to marry the daughter of Felix Fischer in

Klarwill family grave, Döblinger Cemetery, 1898.

Pavilion of the Cycling-Club of the Vienna State and Court Officials, 1898 (from the original drawing).

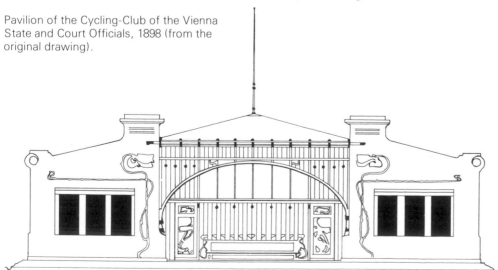

November 1899. It was Fischer, a well-known art patron, and a founder of the Volkstheater, who actually commissioned Olbrich. Drawings dated May and June 1899 exist for the living-room, dining-room, study, drawing-room and bedroom. The interiors were characterised by a distinctive colour scheme and Olbrich's subdivision of the large rooms into smaller, more intimate areas.

Another of Olbrich's interior schemes, also executed in 1899 and considered as more successful, was for David Berl, a coal merchant who had a flat in the Sühnhaus (No. 12) on Vienna's Schottenring. Drawings show Olbrich's studies for the bedroom and music-room (2 versions), the latter being particularly interesting. Ludwig Abels wrote that '. . . the blue music-room is an unprecedented sensation, an intense mystical feeling surrounded us in this room'. (Ludwig Abels, 'Josef M. Olbrich', *Das Interior* II, October, 1901.)

Hermann Stöhr house and shop, 1899, facade and ground floor plan (from the original drawings).

Villa Stift, interior modifications, 1899: *(above)* perspective sketch of the 'Damenzimmer' and photograph of the cupboard as executed, *(below)* window elevation of the dining-room (from the original drawing) and perspective sketch.

Olbrich was also given the commission for an estate of houses on the Hohe Warte, the exclusive hillside at the edge of the Vienna woods, where he hoped to design not only the individual buildings but also their contents and all aspects of their setting. However he left for Darmstadt before this could be realised, so responsibility for the scheme was given to Josef Hoffmann and it became his first major architectural commission. Occupants of the houses included Koloman Moser and Carl Moll (who later sold his house to Gustav Mahler), and friends of the Secession, Hugo Henneberg and Dr Friedrich Spitzer, the art photographer. In 1899 Olbrich had modernised the interiors of Spitzer's flat on the Schliefmühlgasse, and in 1901 these were transferred to his new home on the Hohe Warte, providing an interesting contrast to the strong rectilinear logic of Hoffmann's exterior.

Olbrich's move to Darmstadt in August 1899 occurred at such a time that he was in the unique position at the 1900 Paris Exhibition of being responsible for both an Austrian and a German contribution. His 'Wiener Zimmer' was part of the official Austrian section and was designed to include examples of the work of many of Vienna's artists and craftsmen. Described as the 'Kajutenraum einer Lustyacht' (Cabin of a pleasure yacht), the interior embodied the 'total room' concept which had been advocated by the Secession.

David Berl apartment, interior modifications, 1899: *(right)* bedroom wall elevation (from the original drawing), *(below)* three elevations in the music room (from the original drawing).

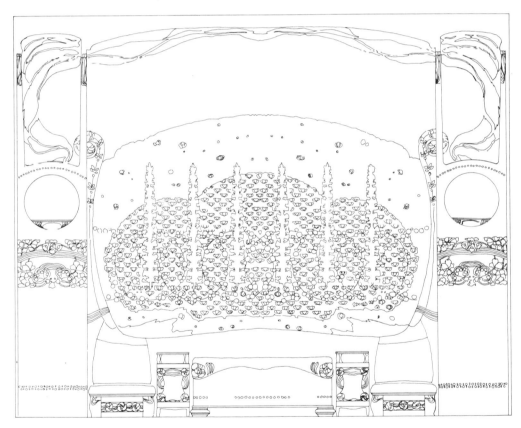

'Wiener Zimmer' at the 1900 Paris Exhibition:
(opposite) tour interior elevations (from the
original drawings), *(right)* contemporary
photographs, *(below)* interior perspective.

CAFÉ NIEDERMEYER

In the summer of 1898, Olbrich produced a number of preliminary drawings for a new café in his home town of Troppau for Leopold Niedermeyer. The site was on a street corner, and Olbrich's design contained shops on the ground floor with the café on the first floor. At the time he was also working on the drawings for an apartment block on a corner site in Vienna for Otto Wagner, the Linke Wienzeile 38, and the Café Niedermeyer scheme bears an interesting comparison. The handling of the corner is remarkably similar, though Olbrich's design is less formal and more inventive in detail; his plans were soon abandoned, although Niedermeyer did eventually build an alternative scheme for the café on the site.

'The planning and building of a café is one of the most rewarding tasks for a modern architect to deal with. The nature of this establishment, particularly common in Austria, has taken on important peculiarities that are eagerly snatched up by the modern art movement, in order to delight and equally to educate the guest with the whole essence of their new young character. The old models according to which café design to date has been copied and thrown together are outdated, and the manager of such a modern establishment who thinks up to date and feels up to date cannot possibly have old junk motifs, still only the result of the architect's lack of ideas (the source of all architectural crimes), used for the construction and decoration of a new home. New modern art, which by means of this one true principle has made possible the conquest of truth in art, is striving to make the essence of the establishment clear in every tiny detail, and from day to day the rift grows greater between the Artist-Architect with his fresh creative genius, with his abundance of purpose-expressing forms, and the architect with the library of clumsy forms which he eagerly copies with tracing-paper and carefully pieces together. On the one side the young creative artistic talent, on the other side the motif-copiers and tradition-idolisers!'

'These staggering words provide the basis for the following observations. For most people a café is a need at a particular hour. There are a thousand reasons that induce people to take up a place to think about and discuss a thousand subjects. One must therefore make provisions to meet these many requirements. The chair, the table, the armchair, the bench, tableware, servants, the space, everything must be explored to ascertain the shape and style in which the desires can be met. The chair for reading the daily paper will be constructed differently to that required for relaxation. Light, air and colours in the room should give a serene feeling, small areas with subdued lighting to make you feel cosy etc. Cleanliness in all parts to enhance and encourage a comfortable feeling. Numerous small ideas could be mentioned which are combined in the mind of a modern architect, to create a piece of work that, in its completeness, fulfils everything, pleases everyone. Above all function, then beauty, and both achieved with modest means. The sketches before you arose from these ideas, and actually explain better than the following enclosed words.'

'As the café was to be located on the first floor, an attempt has been made to strongly attract the attention of the pedestrian and visitor by means of the elaborate facade design. The entrance lobby with the staircase and the adjacent room on the left are a consistent entity and all belong to one interior; the stairs themselves should attractively and without effort, one could say, lead upwards automatically. Above we reach the focal point of the establishment, a charming salon in red, with iron-work bays with a painted cathedral glass frieze, toned darker than the Herrencafe, bathed in light, with billiards and games rooms, and the soft blue-green Damensalon. The whole scene is only divided by function, otherwise everything is in an open layout. The service rooms are located towards the yard with their own staircase and lifts to use the ground floor as business premises; sumptuous flats on the second and third levels. The drawings, mainly perspective elevations, give an impression of the scheme which is still to be

Café Niedermeyer project, Troppau, 1898: *(below)* preliminary sketch, *(opposite)* ground and first floor plans (from the original drawings) and perspective sketch (see also colour plate, page 20).

40

developed to an advanced stage by diligent work and enthusiastic study. As a condition for the artist, the character of the building cannot be achieved by its construction alone, in addition the smallest object, down to the match-holders, must embody the ''educational'' value of modern taste and, as the simplest is always the cheapest to achieve, beauty is associated with simplicity, beautiful and new! With these words I shall close!' (Joseph M. Olbrich, handwritten text dated Vienna, July 7th, 1898.)

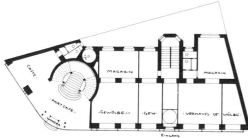

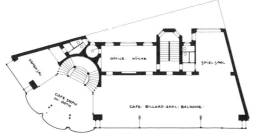

VILLA FRIEDMANN

'His fastidiousness knew no borders, so from his hands arose a formal delicatessen style, and the Viennese memorial will remain the Villa Friedmann in the Vorderbrühl.' (Ludwig Hevesi, 'Josef M. Olbrich', *Altkunst-Neukunst, Wien 1894-1908,* Vienna, 1909.)

Olbrich's first major private commission was for the industrialist Max Friedmann and his wife Johanna, whose country house in the Vienna suburb of Hinterbrühl had been under construction since April 1898. He was asked to take over responsibility for completion of the house from Ludwig Schöne, the original architect, and in doing so was to alter radically both the exterior and interiors from the intended traditional 'Landhaus' style to a 'Secession' style. Olbrich simplified the elevations, eliminating much of the decoration, particularly from the window frames and cornices. He also added a porch and designed every aspect of the interiors. Adolf Böhm collaborated with him on a number of items of ornamentation. The house has been restored to something like its original form.

Villa Friedmann, Hinterbrühl, 1898: *(left)* preliminary sketch for the elevation alterations (from the original drawing) and contemporary photograph of the executed modifications.

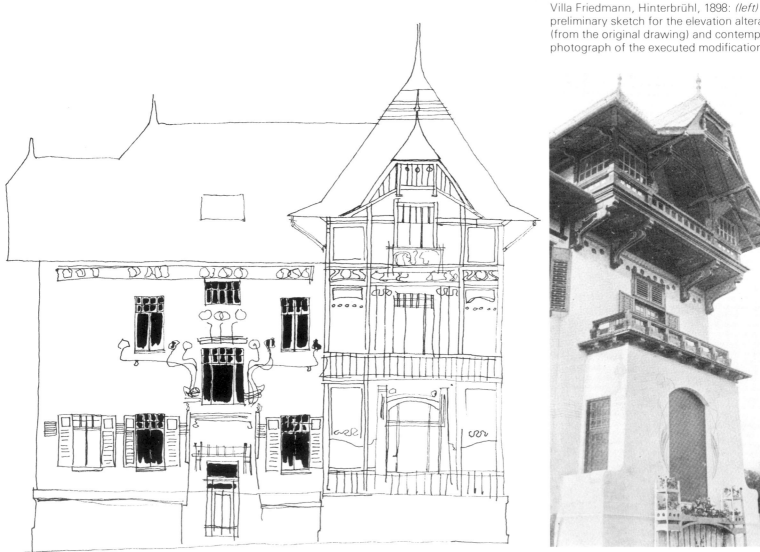

Above
Frau Johanna Friedmann at the open porchway.

Right
Two views of the master bedroom.

Below
Dining-room.

Bottom
Children's room.

Frau Johanna Friedmann's room: perspective
(from the original drawing) and contemporary
photograph of the completed interior.

Contemporary photographs of the main staircase.

HAUS BAHR

'And do you remember last year when we stood on the hill at St. Veit? It was autumn and you were plotting out the site for my house. Far below lay the city, smoke and mist swirling around the gardens, here everything is pure and free. And we stood and looked across to the Hungarian mountains and in the quiet hour we discussed wishes and hopes and worries. The conversation covered the future of art in our fatherland and how we could protect the young from mistakes. And I can still hear you today, as you said in your strong and clear voice: "Style! English! Secession! These are foolish words! Everyone should do what he feels, exactly how he feels — then time will surely show what he is worth!"' (Hermann Bahr, 'Meister Olbrich. In Froher Bewunderung,' *Secession*, Wien 1900, VII.)

In 1899 Hermann Bahr (1863-1934), writer and enthusiastic supporter of the Secession, commissioned Olbrich to design a residence on the hillside at Ober St. Veit to the west of Vienna. A preliminary indication of the Haus Bahr was provided in Olbrich's small sketches entitled *Ein kleines Haus* (A small house), drawn a year earlier in 1898. Olbrich adapted this for the Haus Bahr by reversing the plan arrangement and revising the room types to suit Bahr's requirements. He experimented with a number of design variations and finally sent the completed drawings from Darmstadt in September 1899.

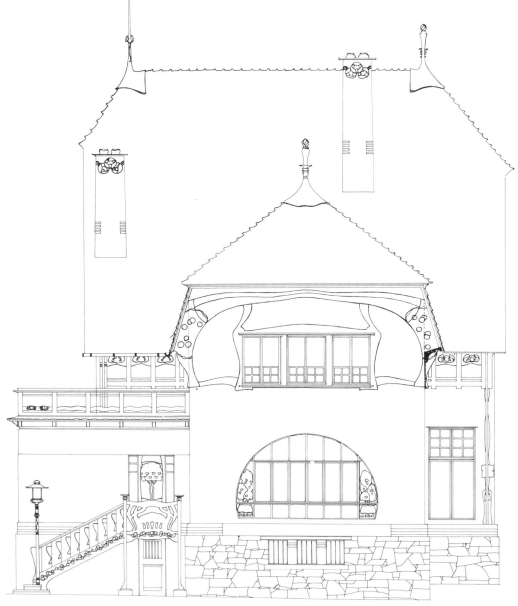

Haus Bahr, Ober St. Veit, Vienna, 1899: *(left and opposite)* north-east and north-west elevations (from the original drawings).

Sketch for 'A small house', 1898.

'It is a real house in the country, in the Viennese countryside, where village and town mingle together. No imitation Swiss cottage, and also no Italian villa, no mansard mansion from Meudon and no chalet from Trouville, and least of all a German Knight's castle . . . It really seems that it has grown from the living earth, like the farmhouses and acacia trees.' (Ludwig Hevesi, *Acht Jahre Secession,* p.512.)

Bahr proudly enthused: 'Just come and see my roof! How faithfully and sincerely the protecting, the sheltering, the maternal nature of the roof is felt here, plain and simple as only the soul of a threatened German peasant can comprehend.' (Hermann Bahr, 'Ein Brief an die Secession', *Ver Sacrum* IV, 1901, pp.227-8.)

The steeply pitched, half-hipped roof was certainly the dominant feature of the Haus Bahr. Covered in dark red tiles and lines of green glass, the roof was anchored at the sides by wooden 'branches', painted green with red fruit, which sprouted from ground level up to the eaves. From the large semi-circular window in the dining-room, the north-east view towards the city could be appreciated. In his study Bahr displayed Klimt's *Nuda Veritas* (dated 1899 and shown at the 4th Secession Exhibition). He occupied the house until 1912, and although much of the original exterior has been lost and the interiors have been radically altered following wartime damage, the Haus Bahr remains recognisable today (Winzerstrasse 22, Vienna XIII.)

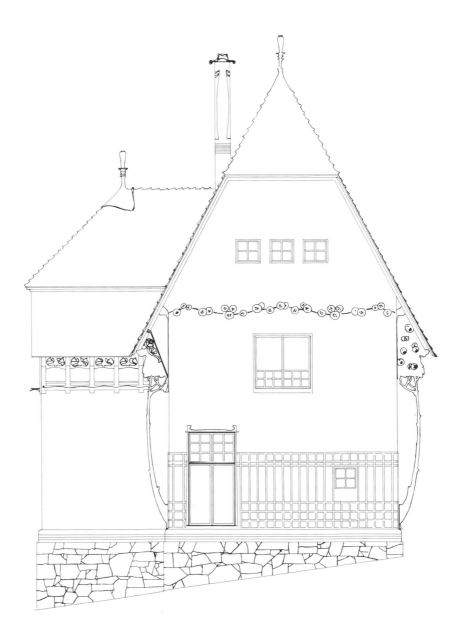

DARMSTADT ARTISTS' COLONY

ESTABLISHMENT OF THE COLONY

'We must build a town, a whole town! Nothing else will do. The authorities will give us a field, in Hietzing or on the Hohe Warte, and then we will create a world there. It means nothing if somebody builds merely one house. How can it be beautiful when there's an unsightly one beside it? What's the use of three, five, ten beautiful houses when the street layout isn't beautiful? What's the use of a beautiful street with beautiful houses if the chairs inside them aren't beautiful or if the plates aren't beautiful? No—a field; otherwise nothing can be done. An empty wide field; and there we will then demonstrate what we are capable of; throughout the layout and down to the last detail, everything controlled by the same spirit, the streets and the gardens and the palaces and the huts and the tables and the chairs and the lamps and the spoons, expressions of the same feeling, but in the middle, like a temple in a sacred grove, a house of work, artists' studios together with craftsmens' workshops, where the artists would now always have the calm and ordered crafts, and the craftsmen would always have the liberated and purging art close at hand, until both would, so to speak, grow together as a single person.' (Hermann Bahr, *Ein Dokument deutscher Kunst*, 1901, p.6.)

Joseph Maria Olbrich and his colleagues had expressed this wish in Vienna, and only six months after the completion of the Secession building Olbrich received an invitation offering him the opportunity of fulfilling the dream. It came from Ernst Ludwig, Grand Duke of Hesse in Germany (1868-1937, ruled 1892-1918), who was establishing an artists' colony in his capital of Darmstadt. So Olbrich left behind his newly acquired commission for an estate of houses on the Hohe Warte for Josef Hoffmann, and moved to Darmstadt to take up the more challenging task.

Olbrich probably first visited Darmstadt in May of 1899 on a tour including Karlsbad, Königswart, Darmstadt and Munich, and Ernst Ludwig was undoubtedly acquainted with the activities of the Vienna Secession from his frequent informal visits to the Austrian capital. The Grand Duke was also familiar with the contemporary English ideas of William Morris and the Arts and Crafts movement; Queen Victoria of England was his grandmother and Ernst Ludwig stayed with her on a number of occasions. In 1897 he had invited M. H. Baillie Scott and C. R. Ashbee, two of the leading English designers, to decorate the reception and dining-room of the Neue Palais in Darmstadt for his first wife Victoria Melita. The schemes were illustrated in the *Innendekoration* magazine in 1899, marking the breakthrough of the English concepts of interior design in Germany.

Economic considerations were, without doubt, significant in Ernst Ludwig's decision to set up an artists' colony in his capital. He wished to improve the quality and update the design of Hessian arts and crafts and stimulate the demand for them, both within and outside Hesse, by making the public more receptive to the 'new' art. The members of the colony were to set the standards by their direct example and by teaching local artists and craftsmen.

The 'Darmstädter Zimmer' displayed by the Artists' Colony at the 1900 Paris Exhibition, perspective sketch (with a model of the Haus Bahr) and contemporary photograph.

The existence in Darmstadt of the art publisher Alexander Koch, who was sympathetic to the new artistic directions, helped to prepare the way for the establishment of the colony. Through his marriage Koch had inherited a carpet manufacturing company, and in 1888 he founded the *Deutsche Tapetenzeitung* to aid their publicity. Its success resulted in his introducing further journals, *Innendekoration* (1890) and *Deutsche Kunst und Dekoration* (1897), which were to play an important role in advertising the activities of the artists' colony. Koch's relationship with Olbrich, however, was never particularly cordial; from the outset he considered the Viennese designer as a 'foreigner' and the paucity of coverage in Koch's magazines of Olbrich's individual work, even compared to that of other colony members, becomes increasingly noticeable. Indeed, in Koch's illustrated catalogue of the 1902 Turin Exhibition, Olbrich is only briefly mentioned and none of his exhibits are illustrated.

The formal establishment of the Darmstadt Artists' Colony took place on July 1st, 1899 with the arrival of the sculptor Rudolf Bosselt (1871-1938) and the painter Hans Christiansen (1866-1945) from Paris and of the decorative painter Paul Bürck (1878-1947) and the industrial and interior designer Patriz Huber (1878-1902) from Munich. Ten days later they were joined by Joseph Olbrich, and finally on July 21st the sculptor Ludwig Habich (1872-1949) and the painter and graphic artist Peter Behrens (1868-1940) arrived from Munich. Christiansen and Habich had held an exhibition of their work in Darmstadt in the autumn of 1898, and Behrens had first exhibited in the city in June 1899.

The seven colony members, whose ages ranged from just twenty up to thirty-three, were given provisional studios in the Porzellanschlösschen by the north exit of the Herrngarten in Darmstadt, and their initial task was to make preparations for an interior scheme to be shown at the 1900 Exhibition in Paris. Discussions began as soon as the colony had been set up, and the *Darmstädter Zeitung* of July 20th 1899 reported that the room would be 'like a fine middle-class reception room'. This 'Darmstädter Zimmer' (Darmstadt Room) was to include examples of the work of all the colony members, although Olbrich produced the overall design for the room. Hans Christiansen was responsible for the large three section stained-glass window. The room was opened to the public several days after the start of the main exhibition on May 15th, and was praised for its simplicity, unity and lack of pretensions in comparison with the great majority of exhibits; the 'Darmstädter Zimmer' was awarded a Gold Medal.

EIN DOKUMENT DEUTSCHER KUNST

As early as 1897 Grand Duke Ernst Ludwig had intended to set up an artists' colony on the Mathildenhöhe, a small hill to the east of the city centre. Grand Duke Ludwig II, who ruled from 1830 until 1848 had purchased the hill, the site of gardens and a former vineyard, and named it after Mathilda, his Bavarian daughter-in-law. In 1880 the municipal reservoir was constructed on the crown of the hill and it still remains in use today. Grand Duke Ernst Ludwig built an ornate Russian Chapel, designed by Benois, on the Mathildenhöhe in 1898; Alice von Hesse had married the Tsar of Russia and a local Orthodox church was needed. In 1899 the architect K. Hoffmann drew up plans for the erection of a number of civic buildings on the hill, which entailed the retention of the reservoir, the chapel and the Platanenhain, the regular plane-tree grove that had been planted in 1898 to replace the former gardens. The Grand Duke, nevertheless, used his influence to reserve the Mathildenhöhe for his artists' colony.

On November 25th 1899 plans were announced for the first major exhibition of the colony, to be held in 1901 under the title 'Ein Dokument Deutscher Kunst' (A Document of German Art), where the colony itself was to form the basis of the display. Bosselt summed up the intentions for their 'Athens' on the Mathildenhöhe: 'an harmonic, pervasive basic feeling, that has its origin in the intellectual qualities, life-feeling and life-direction of the inhabitant'. (Rudolf Bosselt, 'Aufgaben und Ziele der Künstlerkolonie in Darmstadt', *Dekorative Kunst*, 1901, p.443.) The dream of making daily life an aesthetic experience could become a reality, whilst the buildings, considered down to the last detail, would be the exhibition objects in themselves. Financial backing for the venture came from the Grand Duke and, through his influence, from Darmstadt city funds. For the initial two years of the colony's existence, an annual total salary of 16,000 Marks was allocated. This was distributed between the members as follows: Olbrich 4,000 Marks, Christiansen 3,600 Marks, Behrens 3,600 Marks, Habich 1,800 Marks, Bosselt 1,200 Marks, Bürck 900 Marks, Huber 900 Marks. For the 1901 Exhibition a grant of 30,000 Marks was given by the city, a controversial decision that inevitably gave rise to much local resentment against the 'modern' artists.

Joseph Olbrich's natural charm and exuberance, as well as the amicable relationship he quickly developed with the Grand Duke, soon helped establish him as the unelected leader of the Darmstadt Artists' Colony. This later became a source of aggravation within the colony and was one of the factors that led to the departure of several of the members. Olbrich was the only architect among the founder members of the colony (Behrens was still a painter at this time), and so he was entrusted with the architectural aspects of the 1901 Exhibition. In fact, for the next eight years, the colony effectively became Olbrich's private ground for architectural experimentation, with generous financial support and without any imposed aesthetic limitations from his patron.

'At last a small, enthusiastic community, willing to work, in a town that is fortunate to possess neither a ''Glass-palace'' nor an Academy, and doubly fortunate, therefore, because it also lacks the confined norms and standards of our fine art. The open grass, the flowering field, a land where the great labour-pains of a new art were known only from hearsay. Not the battlefield itself, where the intensive struggle between old and young still persists, rather, a field, where free feelings can be peacefully thought out and furthermore can be built . . . Free from all associations, free from all regards and obligations to Art Ministries, free from the quarrel between old and new, trusting in a simply perceiving people, and from their strength these ideas will take a form that doesn't correspond to today's usual sort, but moves far ahead and embraces the future . . . The Colony must

Dress design for the Darmstädter Spiele, the theatrical production at the 1901 Exhibition.

Preliminary sketch of a house for the Artists' Colony, 1899 (from the original drawing). The tilted glazed window became a feature of the Haus Habich.

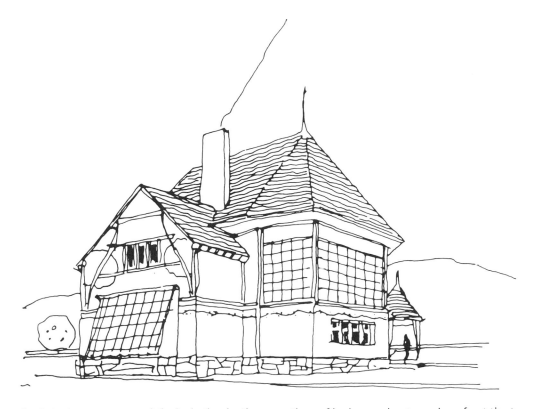

find their purpose and their duties in the creation of independent works of art that help express a happy ''life-principle'' with the greatest feeling and simplicity. A wide terrain, rich in trees and flowers, the Grand Duke's Mathildenhöhe, provides the plan. Up on the highest strip of land the House of Work will be built; there it will be like a temple, with work as the holy service. Eight large ateliers with small master-apartments, a small theatre, gym and fencing halls, guest rooms, showers and baths are all provided in a long building. On the sloping land: the homes of the artists, a peaceful place, to which, after a hard day's work, the artists will come down from the temple of diligence to mix with the people. All the houses will be grouped around a forum with specially laid-out paths, gardens, lamps, fountains and flower beds, all bound in a unity. In the houses themselves, an individual ''Wohnprinzip'' [Living-principle]. The large room (as a room for living) is totally comfortable. There art will be presented in plane and form, music can be heard, conversations exchanged, guests received and fine hours will be spent. All the other room forms stress their function in simplest beauty. The bedroom only the place for sleeping, like a quiet evening-song, for eating and drinking a festive and cheerful drinking song room, the bathroom as sparkling purity. Underneath the roof, the whole is a series of moods. For all that, the useability is never forgotten, it is always considered that each piece should express its purpose, that each fulfils its assigned role to achieve the intended effect. To attain this, to create everything, is the specified intention of the courageous, striving spirit, that we so fortunately now find allotted to the work of the colony; the completion of this gratifying and beneficial task: Our next deed!' (Joseph M. Olbrich, 'Unsere Nächste Arbeit', *Deutsche Kunst und Dekoration* VI, p.366.)

ERNST LUDWIG HAUS

Let there be a temple, whispering with prayers
Trembling with a mysterious wave
Of beauty, for which we beg
With continuous fervent supplications.

This poem was read at the solemn Festspiel (festival) held on March 24th 1900 to mark the laying of the foundation stone of the colony's first building, the 'House of Work'. As early as April 4th 1899, the *Darmstädter Tagblatt* had reported the Grand Duke's intention to build an 'Atelier-Gebäude' (Studio Building) as soon as contracts concerning the Mathildenhöhe had been completed, so it was appropriate that the focal centre of the colony should be called the 'Ernst Ludwig Haus'.

Olbrich began work on the design of the building in September 1899 though the final version was not drawn up until the beginning of 1900 and some drawings were not executed until May. Placed high on the southern slope of the Mathildenhöhe, the long horizontal building represented the true focus of the colony, both in terms of its facilities for work and recreation and its imposing position over the colony houses. A series of red and blue brick steps on the axis of the colony layout led up to the dominant central entrance portal of the Ernst Ludwig Haus, in the same distinctive 'omega' shape that Olbrich used in the porch of the Villa Friedmann, and that was to become a characteristic motif of his Mathildenhöhe houses. The portal is flanked by two huge stone statues representing 'Kraft und Schönheit' (Strength and Beauty) in the form of a Man and Wife carved by Ludwig Habich. Two more statues, representing Victory, executed in bronze by Rudolf Bosselt, are placed within the porch above the door. Inscribed on the brow of the portal was a shortened version of Hermann Bahr's statement that had appeared inside the entrance of the Secession building: 'SEINE WELT ZEIGE DER KÜNSTLER, DIE NIEMALS WAR, NOCH JEMALS SEIN WIRD.' (The artist will show his world, which never was, nor ever will be). Around the doorway Olbrich designed a gold stucco decoration of triangles and circles reminiscent of his earlier graphic work for *Ver Sacrum*. Directly inside the porch was an exhibition hall, the Festraum, which was painted with murals by Paul Bürck. 'Science on a par with art. In the middle the spring of life which nourishes both. On the facing panel: "Joy", illustrated in the form of a dance, as the last embodiment of the three great beauties of life. Left to right: the flower and fruit bearers in art and science, accompanied by fantasy.' *(Die Ausstellung der Künstler-Kolonie Darmstadt 1901, Hauptkatalog.)*

Corridors ran from the portal along the full length of the Ernst Ludwig Haus, and were lit by a low horizontal band of casements. Access was thus possible into the eight studios and these were lit by a band of sloping glazing (now removed) running along the length of the north side of the building. These individual studios could be interconnected and, before the completion of the colony members' houses, were occupied by Bosselt, Huber, Bürck and Christiansen (on the left), and Habich, Olbrich and Behrens (on the right). On the lower level were the administrative and recreation rooms (fencing and gymnastics) and apartments that were later used by Bürck and Huber.

The striking south facade of the Ernst Ludwig Haus, its contrasts of solid and void, of the portal and casements, of white plaster and elaborate decoration, its efficiency as a work studio and its relationship to the site make the building remarkably advanced for its date; a true 'Temple of contemporary art'. *(Darmstädter Zeitung,* 15.5.1901.) In 1904 Olbrich added a sculpture studio on the back of the Ernst Ludwig Haus, and in 1951 the exterior of the building was restored close to its original form.

Opposite
Olbrich's poster for the 'Ein Dokument Deutscher Kunst' Exhibition, 1901, based on a stylized facade of the Ernst Ludwig Haus.

Page 54
Details of the entrance portal, stucco decoration, and bronze 'Victory' by Rudolf Bosselt.

Page 55
Contemporary photograph showing detail of south elevation on completion.

UNTER DEM ALLERHOCHSTEN PROTECTORATE
SR KÖNIGL HOHEIT DES GROSHERZOGS VON HESSEN
EIN DOKUMENT DEUTSCHER KUNST—

DARMSTADT
MAI — OCTOBER 1901
DIE AUSSTELLUNG DER
KUNSTLER — KOLONIE

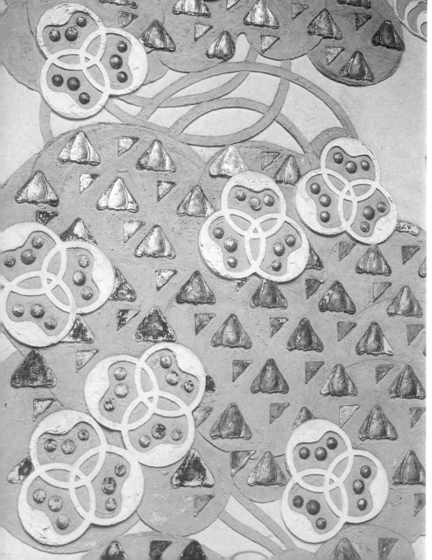

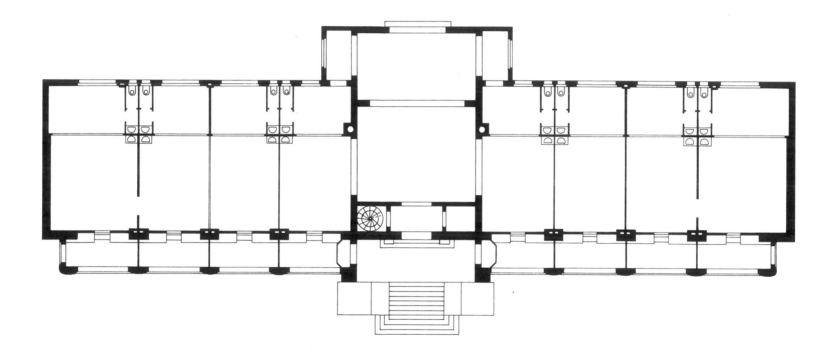

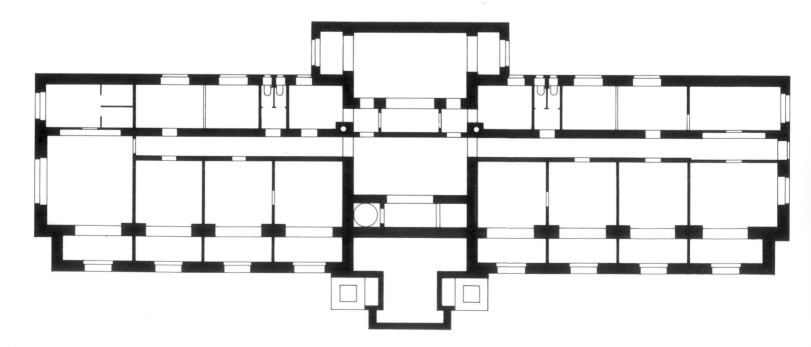

Opposite
South elevation, ground floor and basement
plans (from the original drawings).

Right and below
Perspective section and contemporary
photograph of Olbrich's studio.

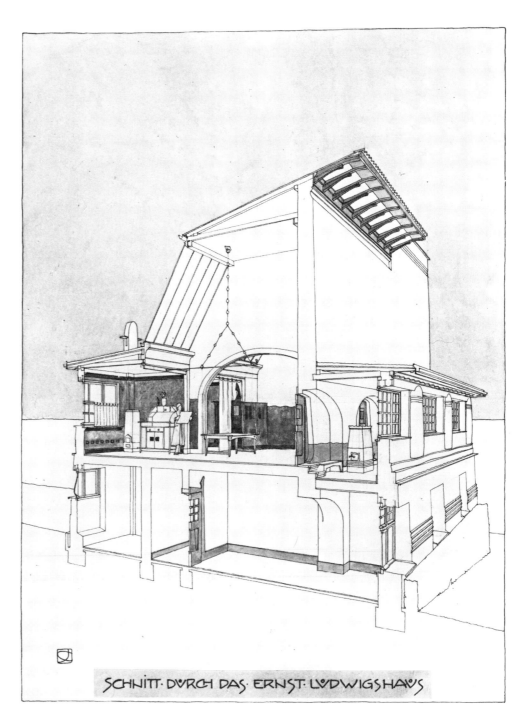

SCHNITT·DVRCH·DAS·ERNST·LVDWIGSHAVS

HAVS OLBRICH

'An Olbrich house is a living organism, and each room in it a living organ.'
(Ludwig Hevesi, Introduction, *Ideen von Olbrich,* Wien, 1900.)

On a triangular site directly in front of the eastern wing of the Ernst Ludwig Haus, Olbrich built his own home. With the exception of the 'Blaue Zimmer' (Blue Room) the Haus Olbrich was opened to the public on May 15th 1901 for the exhibition, although Olbrich himself did not occupy the house until the end of October.

Described by Fritz Schumacher as 'a combination of Vienna and Tunis', the exterior of the Haus Olbrich also recalls the Germanic rural dwellings, yet is adapted in a highly sophisticated manner, particularly in respect of its functionally based asymmetry of composition. The flower gallery on the south face balances the irregular eaves, whilst the open entrance porch opposes a large window lighting the two-storey living-hall, the large multi-purpose room common to most of Olbrich's Mathildenhöhe houses. The whole is bound by a low horizontal frieze of blue and white tiles, a characteristic Secessionstil motif, but which now appears overlayed by a pattern of waving lines.

The internal arrangement centred on the large living-hall almost certainly derives from contemporary English examples, particularly the houses of Baillie Scott. Separated from the hall by a curtain was Olbrich's studio, taking the intended position of the kitchen which was relegated to the basement. The Haus Olbrich earned praise from Alfred Lichtwark for its up to date amenities which included complete water, gas, electricity and heating systems; for a total cost of 75,000 Marks, he considered it to be the least extravagant of the Mathildenhöhe houses.

Although the house is recognisable today, wartime damage and subsequent restoration has altered the roof form and window arrangements quite drastically.

'Here every room has its own special note. Here every detail is harmonious, every trifle ingenious and suggestive. The endeavour to stamp perceptibly upon the exterior of each object a plain relation to its purpose is one of Olbrich's chief

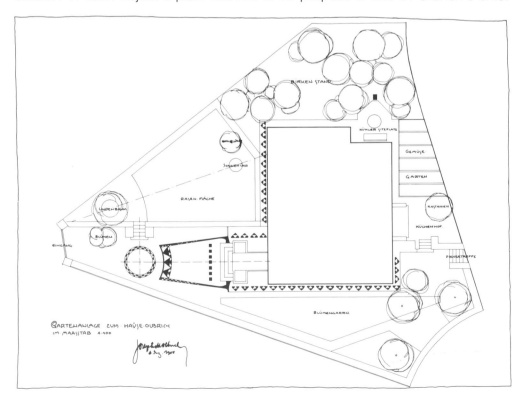

Haus Olbrich, 1900: *(left)* site plan (from the original drawing), *(opposite)* contemporary photograph from the south-west, *(below)* present condition of the house, from the west.

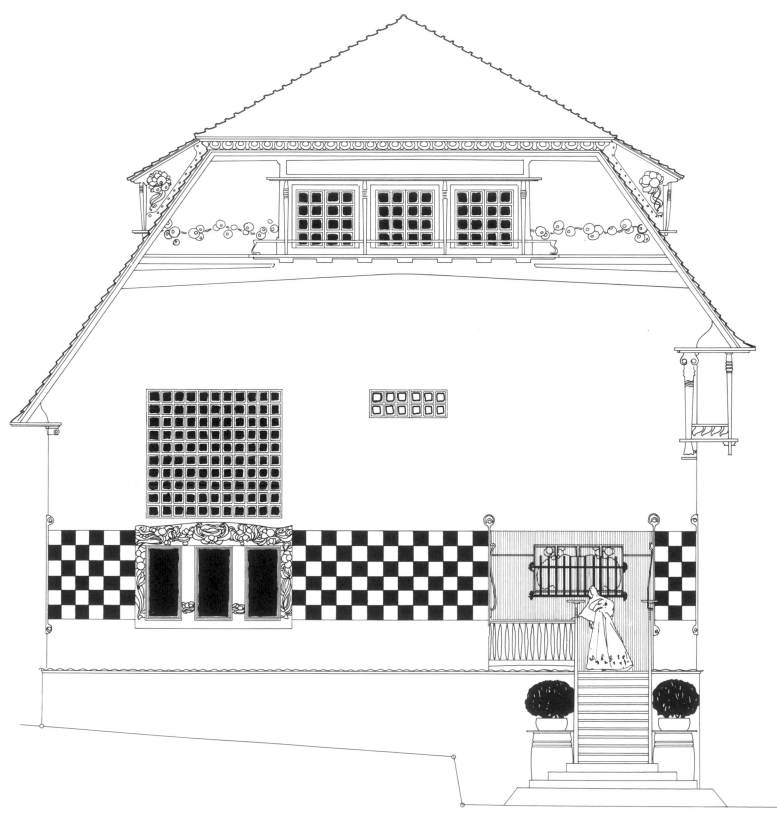

South elevation (from the original drawing).

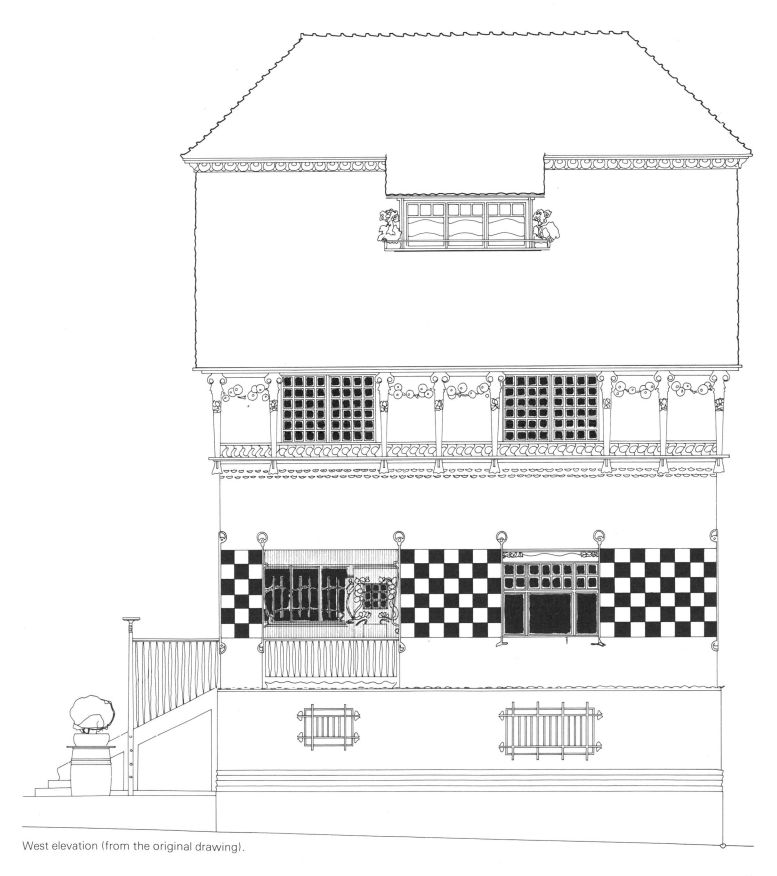

West elevation (from the original drawing).

Service entrance on the east side.

View from the south-east with ornamental fountain designed by Olbrich and sculpture by Ludwig Habich.

characteristics. There is something of the poet in him in his effort to produce harmony. In this way he often (by his colour schemes, for instance) obtains excellent effects, but, of course, he is sometimes betrayed into impossible forms.

'A small flight of steps leads up to Olbrich's house. We find ourselves on the piazetta, which, in accordance with Italian custom, is half room, half open space. To the right a door leads into the dining-room, and on the left into the hall, the living room of the house. The dining-room is bright throughout, the walls white, with delicate golden ornaments — well modelled blossoms crowded together in pyramidal form. The furniture is of cherry wood, highly polished, and of plain design. The sideboard, the principal piece in the room, is adorned with intarsia work and small plaquettes boldly modelled in tinned iron. The light — candles throughout — comes from the walls. The room gains its principal character from a marble fountain, whence issues a continuous stream of water.'

'The great hall to the left of the entrance serves for the social intercourse of the household. The room is intended also to produce effect by its height, extending as it does through two-storeys. It is but sparsely furnished. The stove in the centre — bronze-green oak forming the border for a powerful structure in stone, ornamented with cornelian — is the most attractive feature, and is altogether highly effective. Another bright feature of the hall is a richly-worked curtain,

Right
Front garden and entrance steps to the
'Piazza'.

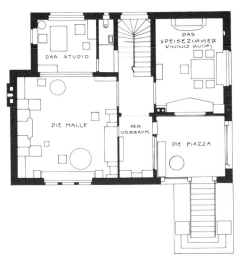

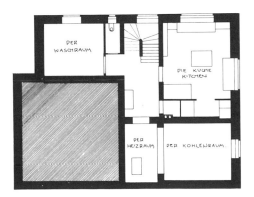

Basement, ground, first and second floor
plans (from the original drawings).

Right
Front garden and entrance steps to the
'Piazza'.

concealing the entrance to the adjoining studio, the walls of which, covered in grey moiré, impart a quiet tone to the room, the large window throwing a full light upon the rich colouring which enlivens the interior. The other colours used are very simple — a green tone for walls and ceiling and a warm lilac for the carpet, the purely geometrical decoration of which is interesting. One observes that Olbrich now frequently employs the simplest linear decorations for wall hangings and tapestries — symmetrically disposed triangles or squares, which have an exceedingly quiet effect. The hall is further brightened by copper receptacles containing flowers, as well as by the lighting from the ceiling, which allows the warm and mellow light to pass through opaque globes. A peculiarity in this room, which I consider excellent, is the placing of the piano. Olbrich is a live artist, and this characteristic appears to be indispensable in the modern architect of interiors, who has not only to satisfy common requirements, but to meet the secret, unexpressed, and delicate desires of highly sensitive men and women. He has very often observed how the pleasure of persons listening to the piano is lessened by looking at the player. He has consequently placed his piano on the level of the first floor, on a projection over the boarding of the entrance door. If we are seated below in the hall, we hear the pure and beautiful sounds come floating down from above, but do not see anything of the technical side of the playing.'

'On the first floor — it seems as if the small and narrow stairs cannot as yet be avoided, but to me they appear great defects in these houses — are the living-room and Olbrich's bedroom, as well as a visitor's room. The colouring of the room, blue and white, is, no doubt, very good. But the form of the furniture, like the ornamentation, is somewhat too stiff, too straight, too linear. A clever expedient is the distribution of the blue ornamentation on walls, doors, etc., in such a manner that it covers those parts which in their frequent use are exposed to touches by the hand, under which white, of course, would have suffered.'

'The chief colour in the bedroom, which adjoins, consists in the yellow tone of the Sorrentine silk of the bed hangings.' (W. Fred, 'The Work of Prof. J. M. Olbrich at the Darmstadt Artists' Colony', *The Studio* vol. 24, p.91.)

Above, left to right
Entrance staircase, the 'Vorraum' (entrance/staircase lobby) and the 'Studio' annex.

Left
View of the 'Piazza' and front door.

Opposite
The double-height 'Halle', showing the door leading from the 'Vorraum,' with the piano above reached from the first floor landing. The curtained partition leads to the 'Studio'.

Dining-room.

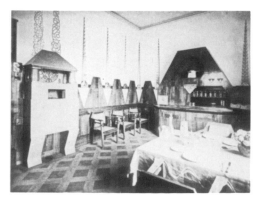

HALLE·IM·HAUSE·OLBRICH· KAMINSEITE
UND·WAND·NACH·DEM·STUDIO

Left and below left
Fireplace wall elevation in the 'Halle' (from the original drawing) and contemporary photograph of the fireplace as executed.

Opposite above
The 'Wohnzimmer', the first floor living-room with violet decoration on the white furniture and walls.

Opposite below
The 'Rote Zimmer', the red guest-room with red-stained woodwork.

Contemporary photograph of the bathroom.

HAUS CHRISTIANSEN

'No modern commonplace house will be shown here, no everyday person will live here, but one who has created his own world and his nest in accordance with his likes and his individuality.' *(Die Ausstellung der Künstler-Kolonie Darmstadt 1901, Hauptkatalog.)*

On the south slope of the Mathildenhöhe, immediately below the Ernst Ludwig Haus, the prime positions were reserved for the houses of Olbrich himself and, on the west side, of Hans Christiansen. Olbrich's drawings for the Haus Christiansen date from spring 1900, and the design seems to have been more of a collaborative effort between architect and occupant than was the case for the other colony

South elevation (from the original drawing).

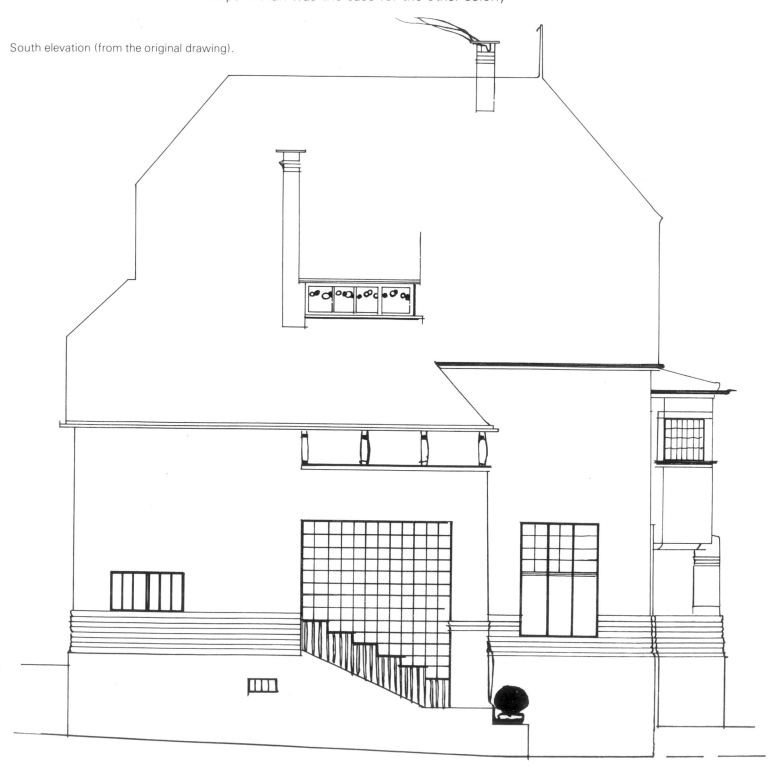

View from the east.

East elevation (from the original drawing).

buildings. Some confusion has no doubt arisen from a caption in *The Studio* (XXIV, 1902, p.269) which illustrates the 'House designed by Hans Christiansen'. In the 1901 Exhibition catalogue, however, Christiansen states: 'Layout and architectural form of the Villa "In Rosen" were drawn by Prof. Olbrich according to my ideas. In addition he designed the four ground floor rooms, whilst the kitchen was designed by Patriz Huber. All other rooms, all items of furniture, and generally all the colouring and decorative ornamentation of the house are by myself . . .' *(Die Ausstellung der Künstler-Kolonie Darmstadt 1901, Hauptkatalog.)* Christiansen particularly emphasised the important role played by the colours in his house: 'the snow white walls interrupted by rich glass-mosaic and red wood engravings, the roof light-green with a violet pattern'. *(Darmstädter Zeitung,* 6.8.1901.) The projecting bay on the east side of the Haus Christiansen, facing the Haus Olbrich, was decorated in bright colours by Christiansen, the central panel depicting a naked man and woman.

GROSSES GLÜCKERT HAUS

The Grosses Glückert Haus (Glückert Haus I), through careful restoration in 1965, bears perhaps the closest resemblance to its original form of all Olbrich's houses. Originally intended as a private house for Julius Glückert, the owner of a Darmstadt furniture factory, the Grosses Glückert Haus was used an an exhibition building for the products of the Glückert Fabrik. The decision to change the use was made shortly before completion of the house, and Julius Glückert himself moved into the adjacent Kleines Glückert Haus, which had been built for the colony member Rudolf Bosselt.

Olbrich worked on the design of the Grosses Glückert Haus on and off for the twelve months from April 1900, though during the latter half of 1900 he was primarily concerned with the Kleines Glückert. The house was not completed until seven weeks after the opening of the 1901 Exhibition, and remained in use for several years as a changing exhibition building.

As with all Olbrich's buildings, the relationship to the site was an important generating force on the form of the Grosses Glückert Haus. The dominant axis is parallel to the Alexandraweg, so the entrance facade faces onto an alleyway which leads down the hill at right angles to the road. Again Olbrich has employed the 'omega' porch for the entrance and the area is concentrated with decorative embellishments. The large mural shown on Olbrich's drawing over the portal remained unexecuted, but the stylized trees on the north and south gables and on the east bay, which were completed, are of particular interest.

Internally the Grosses Glückert Haus was arranged symmetrically about the entrance-fireplace axis. The entrance lobby led directly into the central two-storey Halle, passing under a timber gallery. Arched openings in the Halle gave access to the staircase and the fireplace bay. In 1908 Olbrich redecorated the house, the new scheme providing a distinct contrast to the original and underlining the development of the architect's later work.

The Kleines and Grosses Glückert houses, present condition.

Opposite
North gable of the Grosses Glückert Haus facing the Alexandraweg.

Page 72
(above) Grosses Glückert Haus, west entrance portal, *(below left)* Grosses Glückert Haus, fireplace bay, *(below right)* Kleines Glückert Haus, north elevation.

Page 73
Grosses Glückert Haus, contemporary photograph of east elevation with the projecting fireplace bay.

West elevation (from the original drawing).

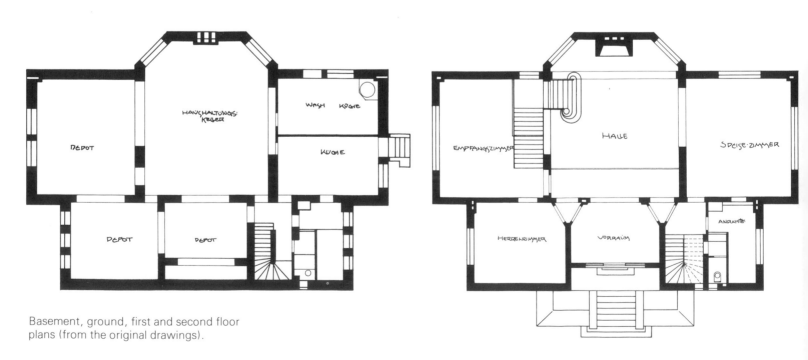

Basement, ground, first and second floor
plans (from the original drawings).

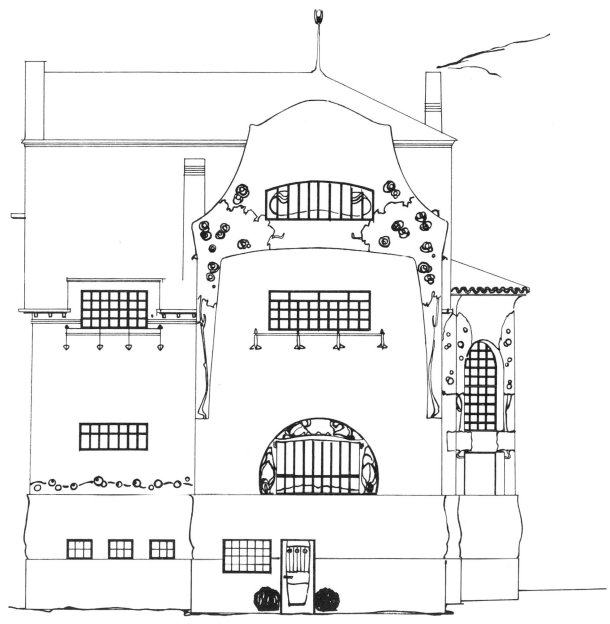

South elevation (from the original drawing).

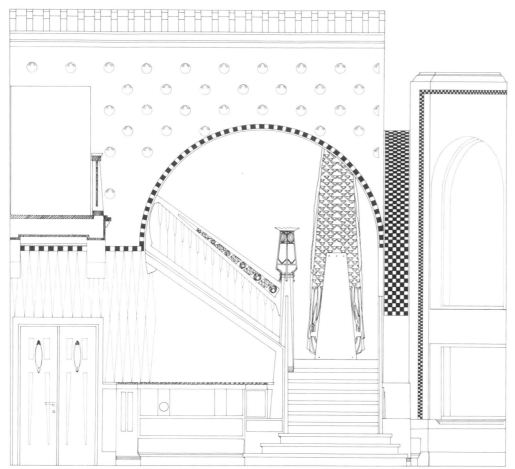

North wall of the Halle with staircase (from the original drawing).

Below left
The central double-height 'Halle'.

Below
The dining-room with service hatch (south of the Halle).

East wall of the Halle with fireplace (from the original drawing).

Below
The 'Herrenzimmer' (north-east of the 'Halle').

Below right
The 'Damensalon/Empfangsraum' (north of the 'Halle').

KLEINES GLÜCKERT HAUS

Noted in some of Olbrich's early drawings as the 'Haus Bosselt', for the colony sculptor, the Kleines Glückert Haus (Glückert Haus II) was occupied by Julius Glückert from 1901 until his death in 1911. Bosselt probably collaborated on the design, which was completed in outline as early as summer 1900 when drawings were published in *Deutsche Kunst und Dekoration*. (No. VI, 1900, p.369.)

The form of the Kleines Glückert Haus bears a close resemblance to that of the Haus Habich, which it faces across the axial path leading down from the Ernst Ludwig Haus. It consists of a similar simple flat-roofed block, but this is surmounted by a barrel vault on the northerly Alexandraweg side. This street frontage is dominated by a projecting bay which forms, on the upper storey, a range of lattice windows set in frames carved by Bosselt; above this is a small balcony. On the front of the barrel, the projection is terminated by a band of windows and a door (providing access from the dining-room to the balcony), with a curving parapet that echoes the gables of the adjacent Grosses Glückert Haus.

Internally the Kleines Glückert Haus was planned in much the same way as the

Contemporary photograph taken on completion of the house in 1901.

Below and opposite
The 'Vorraum' (entrance hall) with decorations by Olbrich; the recessed seat is within the projecting bay on the north elevation.

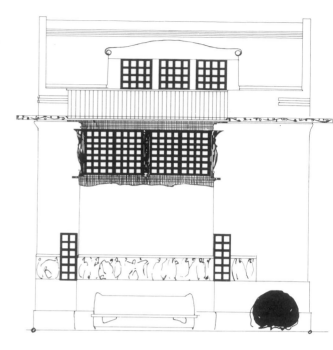

East and north elevations (from the original drawings). The window arrangement and decorations were amended in execution.

Detail of entrance.

Haus Olbrich and, although Olbrich was responsible for decorating the Vorraum (hallway) and part of the stairs, most of the internal arrangements were the work of Patriz Huber. The house was slightly modified in its realisation when the entrance porch on the east elevation was enclosed and the large Halle window was transferred to the south elevation. None of the intended friezes were executed. The Kleines Glückert Haus was restored after war damage and remains close to its original appearance.

Present condition of the Kleines Glückert Haus viewed from the Alexandraweg.

Detail of window bay, with sculpture by Rudolf Bosselt.

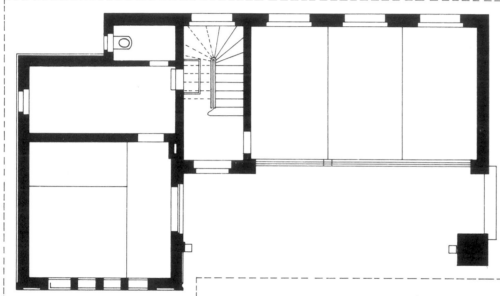

Stable building for Julius Glückert, south and west elevations and plan of the first version, designed 1901-02 (from the original drawings).

Glückert family grave, Alter Friedhof, Darmstadt, 1900.

Stable building for Julius Glückert,
Darmstadt, 1905.

HAUS HABICH

The Haus Habich, designed by Olbrich for the sculptor Ludwig Habich, represented a significant departure from most of Olbrich's other colony houses, bearing a closer resemblance to the Mediterranean dwellings he had sketched on his travels than to any Germanic architectural traditions. A range of early drawings exist for the house, dated around spring 1900, which develop the flat roof theme. This roof, with its wide, overhanging eaves, the simple cubic massing, pierced by windows and doors, and the roof terrace are not dissimilar to some of the houses of Adolf Loos and Le Corbusier. Olbrich, however, emphasised prominent parts of the house by the selective use of decoration. The Haus Habich included a number of highly original features, not least of which was the projecting bay of sloping glazing on the north facade.

Patriz Huber completed the interior designs for the Haus Habich to help relieve Olbrich's work load. The house was almost totally destroyed in the war, and has been rebuilt in an almost unrecognisable form with a pitched roof.

Haus Habich, 1900: contemporary photograph from the north-east.

West and north elevations (from the original drawings).

HAUS KELLER

More conventional in form than the other Mathildenhöhe houses, and perhaps less convincing as an integrated design, was the Haus Keller. Planned as a private home, called 'Beaulieu', the house featured an interesting range of traditional features in combination with some of Olbrich's own invention. The projecting semi-circular bay on the Alexandraweg elevation, for instance, was fused with a doorway surrounded by a 'token' arch. The house also included such diverse elements as a circular window and quasi-mediaeval half-timbering at the upper levels.

Unlike most of the other colony houses, the Haus Keller had no central two-storey Halle, the living-room being confined to a single level. During the 1901 Exhibition the house was used to display the products of various Darmstadt firms. Severe wartime damage and subsequent rebuilding have left the house almost unrecognisable today.

Haus Keller, 1900: contemporary photograph from the south-west.

Opposite
View from the Alexandraweg, with the Exhibition Gallery beyond.

Detail of the staircase entrance bay on the north elevation.

West elevation (from the original drawing).

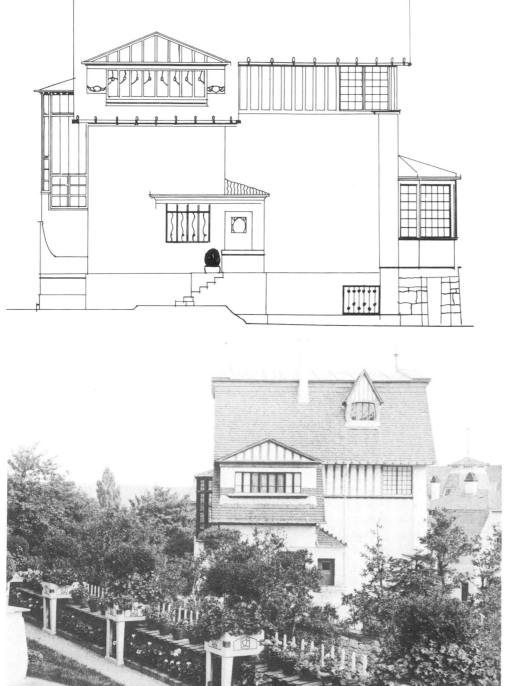

Contemporary photograph from the entrance
path of the Haus Olbrich with Olbrich's
monogrammed flower boxes.

Detail of entrance lobby.

North elevation (from the original drawing).

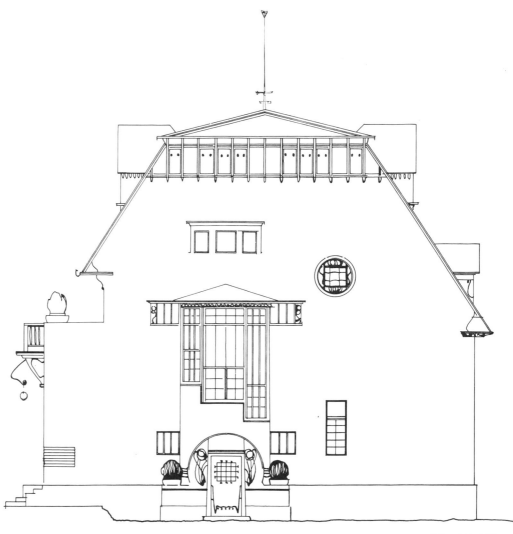

Buffet in the 'Halle'.

South-eastern corner of the 'Halle'.

HAUS DEITERS

The Haus Deiters, built for the colony business leader Wilhelm Deiters, was in the south-east corner of the colony's allotted area at the junction of Mathildenhöhweg and Victoria-Melita-Weg (now Prinz-Christians-Weg). It was this street corner siting that Olbrich used to generate the overall form of the house. 'The strong turning-point is emphasised by a tower-like structure, attached on both sides on the right corner to two wings along the street frontages, the exterior form of which results from the internal accommodation of the house.' *(Die Ausstellung der Künstler-Kolonie Darmstadt 1901, Hauptkatalog.)*

'Deiters' is a small house, erected at a low cost, and is chiefly noteworthy for the way in which the ground-plan problem has been solved. By avoiding every gangway or corridor, every dead angle in the whole house, the rooms, notwithstanding the small area, have become large. Even the ante-room has been made into a living-room by brown-tinted furniture, built into the walls. The living-room, placed in the outermost left wing, receives its light through a window of three bays, placed obliquely across two fronts, and by this arrangement has been formed into a large interior, in which green furniture, embellished by plain tarsia-work, lightly but broadly designed, produces a very good effect. The dining-room is quite bright, and furnished with natural, unstained, polished wood. Adjoining is a small smoking-room. The first floor contains bedrooms, and the basement, as in other houses, kitchen, bathroom and laundry.' (W. Fred, 'The Work of Prof. J. M. Olbrich at the Darmstadt Artists' Colony', *The Studio* vol. 24, p.98.)

The ground floor rooms of the Haus Deiters were open to the public for the duration of the 1901 Exhibition whilst Deiters occupied the upper rooms. The house remains in relatively good condition today.

South and west elevations (from the original drawings).

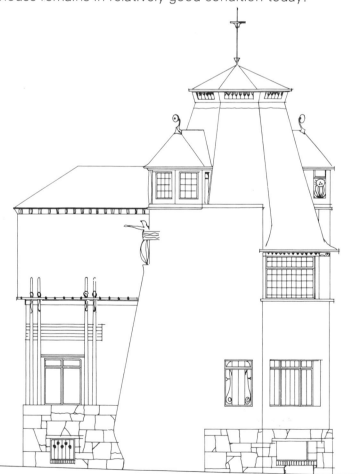

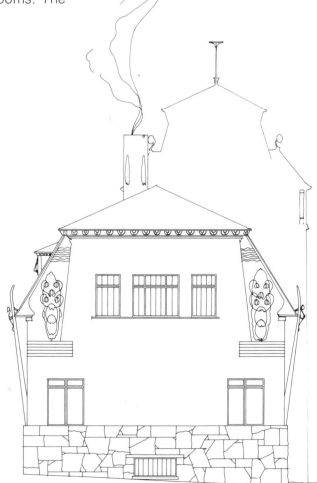

Present condition of the Haus Deiters and
detail of the entrance.

Perspective sketch from the south-east, 1900
(from the original drawing).

PROVISIONAL 1901 EXHIBITION BUILDINGS

The 1901 Exhibition entrance portal was placed on the main approach to the Mathildenhöhe from the centre of Darmstadt directly in line with the Russian Chapel. Olbrich's early sketches show the development of the idea from a massive arched structure, resembling some of his Vienna drawings for memorials and graves, to the final twin towers between which a simple canvas canopy was hung with two panels painted by Paul Bürck on the opposing inner faces of the structures. The original intention was to build a permanent gateway to the colony, but in the event the portal was designed as a temporary structure. The contractor J. W. Diehl began work on the portal on December 1st 1900 and it was finally destroyed on November 25th 1901.

Contemporary photograph of the temporary exhibition Entrance Portal with paintings by Paul Bürck and the Russian Chapel beyond.

Post card kiosk.

Main hall of the restaurant, with stained glass windows by Hans Christiansen.

Shortly beyond the entrance, two small kiosks for the sale of catalogues and postcards were placed; these were also built by Diehl in December 1900.

The Exhibition restaurant was located at the eastern end of the Platanenhain in front of the reservoir. In addition to the timber and plaster structure, Olbrich designed the furniture, linen and cutlery, as well as the china in collaboration with Paul Bürck. Hans Christiansen was responsible for the glassware. The two-level restaurant was built to accommodate 400 people on each floor. These were linked by a central staircase 'so as not to occupy the socially desirable corner positions'. *(Darmstädter Zeitung, 2.5.1901.)*

The hall was 'completely done out in white, with simple ornamental stripes on the walls' *(Darmstädter Zeitung,* 2.9.1901), with a window as its centrepiece depicting Bacchus by Hans Christiansen: 'Not only the largest, but also the boldest composition in Tiffany glass . . . that we have seen to date'. *(Kunst und Handwerk* 51, 1900-01, p.290.) Christiansen had visited Chicago to see Tiffany's work in 1893.

The 'Gebäude für Fläschenkunst', the Exhibition's temporary gallery, attracted much attention during the 1901 Exhibition and continued to do so for years after its demolition. Designed to house paintings and graphic art, the inexpensive timber frame gable structure was simply covered with canvas and plaster and contained adjustable partitions inside. The gallery was positioned on the axis of the colony lay-out facing up towards the Ernst Ludwig Haus. Seven fins attached to each side of the gallery contributed to a visual rhythm rather than serving any structural purpose. Erich Mendelsohn illustrated the gallery in his 1919 lectures, together with Olbrich's Wedding Tower, praising their dynamic expressiveness and how Olbrich had foreseen the future direction even before the introduction of the new materials that were to make it possible. Contemporary opinion was

divided, particularly over the validity of the large expanse of north facing glazing. The *Darmstädter Zeitung* of 23rd May stated 'that one will seldom find paintings exhibited in such favourable lighting conditions'. On September 2nd another writer in the same newspaper claimed 'we are not of the opinion that the method of lighting the whole area with a single large window represents an improvement. The lighting is just not even in all parts of the space.'

Opposite the Haus Behrens, on the north side of the Alexandraweg, was the 'Blumenhaus', the flower house. There was currently a great interest in the beauty of natural objects, particularly the 'Kultus der Blumen', (cult of the flower), and this was closely allied with the florally derived decoration of much Jugendstil design. The Blumenhaus consisted of an unusual but effective combination of elements. Paired projecting arms enclosed a display in the entrance forecourt, their form consistent with the Exhibition entrance portal and the gallery. The entrance proper was marked by a huge gable, not unlike the outline of those on the Grosses Glückert Haus, and a stylized plant frieze surrounded the characteristic circular opening. Behind, the interior displays were housed in a glass pavilion, with five half-octagon 'chapels', appearing remarkably like some of the later expressionist projects of Bruno Taut and Hans Poelzig. Olbrich planned displays in the Blumenhaus that were changed each month: 'Flowering plants in tasteful combination with artistically conceived and executed ornaments — perhaps bronze or pottery — arranged to achieve a highly artistic impact.' *(Die Ausstellung der Künstler-Kolonie Darmstadt 1901, Hauptkatalog.)*

The members of the Darmstadt Artists' Colony, particularly Peter Behrens, considered the theatre to be an essential part of life and that it should be demonstrated as such in the colony. Seen as the highest cultural symbol, the theatre embodied the 'Gesamtkunstwerk' principle — the total work of art. Music, literature, dance, art and design could be brought together in an artistic unity.

It is likely that Olbrich and Behrens visited Hermann Bahr in Vienna in the summer of 1900 to seek advice on the establishment of the theatre, and Bahr may have returned the visit. In the event a full theatre was not built, but the 'Spielhaus'

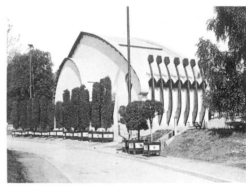

Exhibition Gallery for painting and sculpture (Gebäude für Fläschenkunst), viewed from the north-east and south-east.

Opposite above
Exhibition Gallery, elevation and plan (from the original drawing).

Opposite below
'Blumenhaus', ground plan, perspective and side elevation dated 4th August 1900 (from the original drawing).

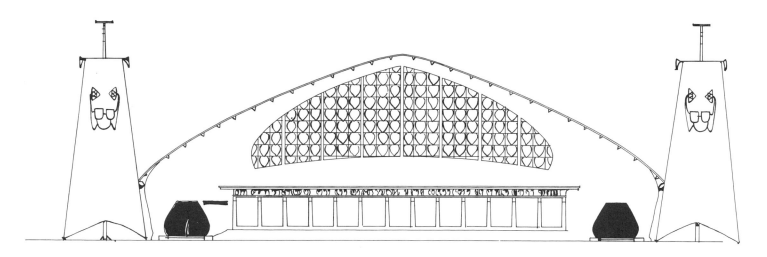

AUSSTELLUNGSGEBÄUDE · FÜR · FLÄCHENKUNST · MAASSTAB 1:200 · VON · PROF · OLBRICH · 1900

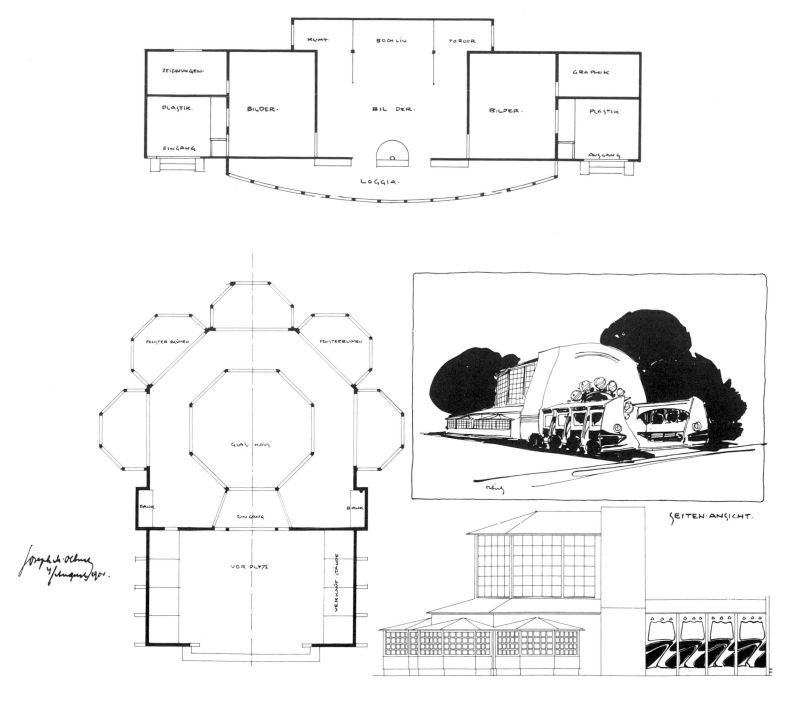

(Playhouse) served to function as such. Olbrich's sketches reveal two main lines of development. The earlier drawings show a composite arrangement with a central seating/stage area surrounded by ancillary rooms. The later scheme, which was built, was much simpler, providing a pitched roof that spanned over the entire building with internal partitions to divide the various functions. The Spielhaus was constructed of timber, plaster and canvas and the interior was enclosed by an undecorated deep violet material formed into the shape of a barrel vault.

At the edge of the Platanenhain, on the northern boundary of the Exhibition area, Olbrich sited the Orchestra Pavilion. The simple A-frame structures sheltered the orchestra platform, which was reached by a staircase and doorway at the back, and two cloakrooms were placed at the sides. The axis of the pavilion was aligned with the grid of the plane trees, so the audience would be seated under the leafy canopy. Guest conductors during the 1901 Exhibition included Carl Stix with the Vienna New Philharmonic Orchestra and Richard Strauss.

One of Olbrich's earliest sketches for a colony building was for a theatre studio, although this never came to fruition. He described the studio in *Architektonischen Monatshefte* of June 1900; it is interesting to note his reference to the building as a 'machine'. 'Intended for the production of large items such as props, curtains, sets, dioramas, a single studio is projected for the site on the Mathildenhöhe allotted to the Artists' Colony. The exterior form arises from the internal requirements: a large, closed back wall with a flush, vertical surface on which the canvas is stretched. In front and to both sides, the light floods in, with the rooms necessary for props, wardrobes and heating, the whole project is a single machine which fulfils all the requirements of the artists. The studio is specially projected for the production of modern theatre decoration and is intended for Herrn Prof. Christiansen. The open hall under the studio, like the connected reception room on the ground floor, is provided for smaller studies up to the large works. The construction cost amounts to 18,000 MK including the mechanical equipment for the hydraulic lowering and raising apparatus.'

Orchestra Pavilion, section, elevations and plan (from the original drawing).

SCHNITT   VORDERANSICHT.   SEITENSICHT.

GRUNDRISS

Right
Theatre studio designed for Hans Christiansen (unexecuted).

Below
Preliminary sketches and contemporary photograph of the 'Spielhaus' as executed.

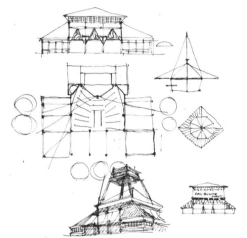

1904 ARTISTS' COLONY EXHIBITION

The financial failure of the 1901 Darmstadt Artists' Colony Exhibition necessitated a drastic reappraisal of the colony's structure. This together with individual discontentment resulted in the departure of Paul Bürck, Hans Christiansen and Patriz Huber in the summer of 1902. (Bürck went to teach at Magdeburg, Christiansen worked in Darmstadt and Paris, and Huber went to Berlin, where he committed suicide in September.) Peter Behrens and Rudolf Bosselt left Darmstadt in 1903 (both went to teach at Düsseldorf), leaving only Joseph Olbrich and Ludwig Habich of the original colony members. Consequently they were joined later in the year by Johann Vincenz Cissarz (1873-1942) from Dresden, Daniel Greiner (1872-1943) from Paris and Berlin, and Paul Haustein (1880-1944) from Munich and Dresden.

The scope of the 1904 Exhibition, held from July 15th until October 10th, was considerably less ambitious than the earlier venture. Olbrich designed a number of temporary buildings, including restaurant and concert pavilions, and the only permanent building — the 'Dreihäusergruppe' (Three House Group). Olbrich had planned to erect a provisional exhibition building, but this was abandoned and the Dreihäusergruppe and the Ernst Ludwig Haus were used to house the exhibits.

The area of the Mathildenhöhe to the south and west of the Haus Behrens was used for the provisional buildings (it had been the site of the Blumenhaus and Spielhaus in 1901), whilst the Dreihäusergruppe was built further to the west on the corner of the present-day Prinz-Christians-Weg and Stiftstrasse. Olbrich's Concert Pavilion was virtually identical to his 1901 Orchestra Pavilion, except that it had an arched opening, rather than following the A-shaped structure. The restaurant pavilions were arranged in a semi-circle, facing the Concert Pavilion to the north, and consisted 'in the main of five round pillared temples of solid timber construction.' (Dekorative Kunst 13, 1905, p.52.) These 'temples' were·mostly open at the sides, and were painted white with green roofs.

The Dreihäusergruppe consisted of three linked houses — the 'Predigerhaus' (Preacher's house) or 'Graue Haus' (Grey house), the 'Blaue Haus' (Blue house)

Dreihäusergruppe, north and west elevations/sections (from the original drawings).

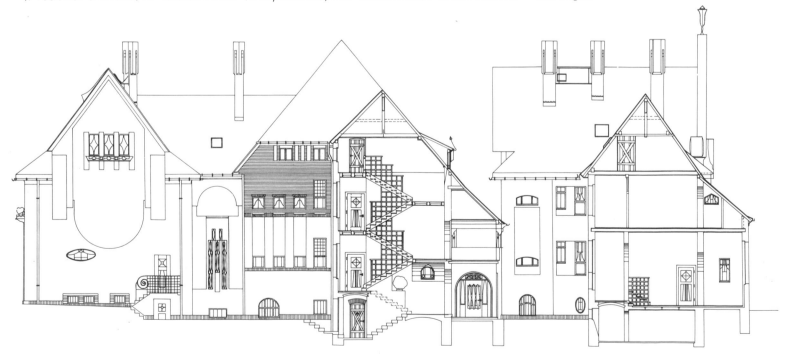

Above, left to right
The Dreihäusergruppe: the Blaue Haus, the Eckhaus and the Graue Haus.

Restaurant and Orchestra Pavilions at the 1904 Exhibition.

and the 'Eckhaus' (Corner house). Seen as 'simple, inexpensive, but artistically designed individual homes' *(Darmstädter Tagblatt,* 19.7.1904), the houses, like the 1901 houses, were intended to demonstrate the individual character of the home and its contents and to stimulate an artistic response from the occupants. Olbrich's drawings for the Dreihäusergruppe date from spring and summer 1903, and construction was started at the end of July. His primary objective with the form was to resolve the conflict between the requirements of housing three families and their need for individual identity. Olbrich achieved this by emphasising three prominent gables, with differing orientation to avoid direct comparison, each with characteristic colouring and detailing.

The Predigerhaus was built for the Grand Duke's court chaplain. The undulating gable was set back from the street and was emphasised by unusual sweeping lines of red sandstone set against a dark grey rough plastered surface. Two seraphims were carved in the sandstone by Greiner, and Habich decorated the bronze door. The Blaue Haus, later sold to the Kommerzienrat (councillor of commerce) Frau Knöckel, was so called for the ground floor that was 'covered with blue glazed bricks that reach up to the underside of the first floor windows'. *(Deutsche Kunst und Dekoration* 14, 1904, p.634.) Above, the white gable surface provided a plain background to the windows below the generous overhang of the roof. The Eckhaus, or 'Holzgiebelhaus' (Timber gable house), later sold to the Count von Büdingen, was sited on the street corner. The gable was characterised by a series of vertical shafts consisting of brickwork at the lower level and continued in timber work above. In front of the house Olbrich designed a projecting bay with a gently curving outline to complement the shallow pitch of the gable above.

The Dreihäusergruppe still exists today, but was heavily damaged in the war, so it retains few of Olbrich's original details.

THE WEDDING TOWER AND EXHIBITION BUILDINGS

'As we are reliably informed, the artists' colony intends to erect an observation tower on the Mathildenhöhe in the direct vicinity of the reservoir, the construction of which will begin in May of this year [1900]. The tower, designed by Herr Professor Olbrich, should reach an overall height of 68 metres. The massive architecturally decorated plinth, which stands 10 metres above the reservoir, ends in a platform which measures 8½ metres square, above which rises the rigid tower that terminates at a height of 43 metres with a second platform, reached by a spiral staircase, from which one enjoys a wide view over the whole district. It measures 6½ metres square and is thought of as a large hall with glazed walls, which will contain painted scenes depicting the history of Darmstadt and in the middle will be an orienting table. At a height of 13 metres above this platform rises a Hesse crown made of red glass and gold, and the whole structure terminates in a flagpole also serving as a lightning conductor. The cost of this very attractive structure, distinguished by its slenderness, amounts to 22-24,000 Mk.' *(Darmstädter Tagblatt, 30.4.1900.)*

This announcement was made in the same month that the Grand Duke had made Olbrich a 'professor', and when plans were being made for the 1901 Exhibition; the tower was to be completed for the Exhibition and its position at the north-eastern corner of the reservoir was indicated on a preliminary site plan. The idea soon had to be abandoned as there were insufficient funds for the construction of such a tower.

On February 2nd, 1905 Grand Duke Ernst Ludwig married his second wife Princess Eleonore von Solms-Hohensolms-Lich, and Olbrich was presented with the opportunity to fulfil his dream to build a tower to complete his 'Athens' with an 'Acropolis'. The city authorities asked him to prepare sketches for a tower on the Mathildenhöhe to commemorate the marriage; it was to be called the Hochzeitsturm (Wedding Tower), although some of Olbrich's drawings were titled 'Eleonorenturm' after the Princess.

Olbrich collaborated closely with the Grand Duke on the design of the tower, and the earliest sketches resembling the distinctive 'Fünf-fingergiebel' (Five-finger gable) date from March 1905. The Grand Duke is said to have favoured the symbol of an outstretched hand, and some sources even claim that it was his own idea, though this seems unlikely. From May of 1905, Olbrich and Ernst Ludwig seemed to agree that the tower should be incorporated with a permanent exhibition building erected on top of the reservoir, and between them they managed to sway the city authorities to the same opinion. Olbrich drew up the plans during February 1906 and presented the scheme for approval on March 1st. The ensuing debate was heated, particularly as the projected cost of 300,000 Marks would necessitate higher taxes, and some committee members felt annoyed at the way the Grand Duke was using his position to influence their decision. The scheme was finally agreed by twenty-eight votes to ten.

'The base line of the building lies on the flat surface of the second terrace and was fixed by means of the sloping path of the earth bank of the high reservoir nearby. On the south-west corner of the hill the staircase, in place of the technically necessary earth bank, leads to the upper forecourt and then links to the pergola, completing the whole building. From a terrace, raised by a few steps, the wide, comfortable stairs lead to the first landing. A canopy-like chapel building rises above this, to supply the building mass with a broad site. Stone supports carry the cross vault, decorated with coloured mosaics, and light arches support the golden pyramid roof. Rest seats are placed on each side of a wall fountain, in the shade of the lofty halls, and from this raised point, one first enjoys the view of the

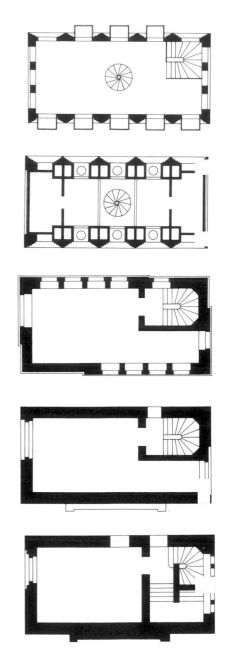

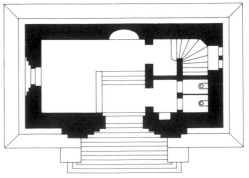

The 'Hochzeitsturm' (Wedding Tower), plans (from the original drawings) and contemporary photograph from the south-west.

AUSSTELLUNGSGEBÄUDE· AUF· DER· MATHILDENHÖHE· MIT· AUSSICHTSTURM·

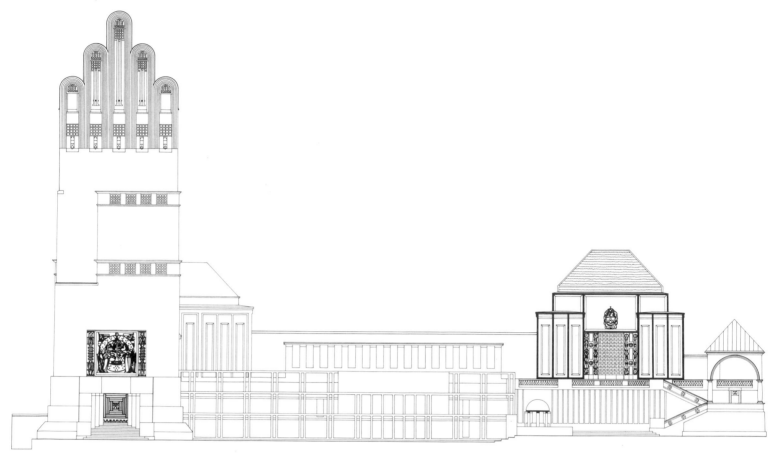

Exhibition Building and Wedding Tower, north elevation (from the original drawing).

site lay-out. The second flight of stairs leads on to the paved uppermost terrace, reaching the level of the old hilltop.'

'The entrance building stands on this plateau. White pillars rising up towards the back frame the large rich oak door. Facetted pieces of glass crystal are distributed like jewels in the square depressions of the timber leaves. On entering the door the barrel-vaulted vestibule comes into view; then, opposite the doorway, the entrance to the exhibition hall. Along the length of the hall, two smaller, high level barrel-vaults cut into the large semi-circle of the hall roof forming small chapels, and on their end walls long windows allow daylight to enter the room. The positions are arranged for exhibition functions, particularly for tall narrow church windows, which are thus provided with an existing suitable surrounding in these chapel-like spaces.'

'On the north side of this hall a five section glass door leads out under the windows to the rose-garden. To the sides of the main door lie on the right a cash-office and the administration rooms, and on the left the cloakroom and a conference room which, if required, can function as a cloakroom. Special attention has been paid in every room to fulfil the exhibitions' technical requirements. A workroom is placed next to the secretary's room, from where the exhibits can be distributed among the halls.'

'A hoist is provided to lift works from the flat area of the large depot on the approach drive up to the height of the exhibition halls. Laden vehicles can drive directly up to this aforementioned depot room, the particular pieces can easily be unloaded for the exhibition. The unpacking of crates, the preliminary inspection and observation of the condition of arriving works, the crate storage and freight dispatch will be dealt with in these rooms. For further handling, the pieces are taken in the lift and are distributed to their assigned places from the upper workroom. Two separate toilets are accessible from the vestibule. The severe formal simplicity of the hall is particularly intensified by the quiet colour treatment

Preliminary sketches for the Exhibition Building entrance pavilion (from the original drawings).

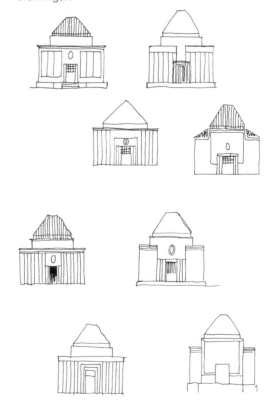

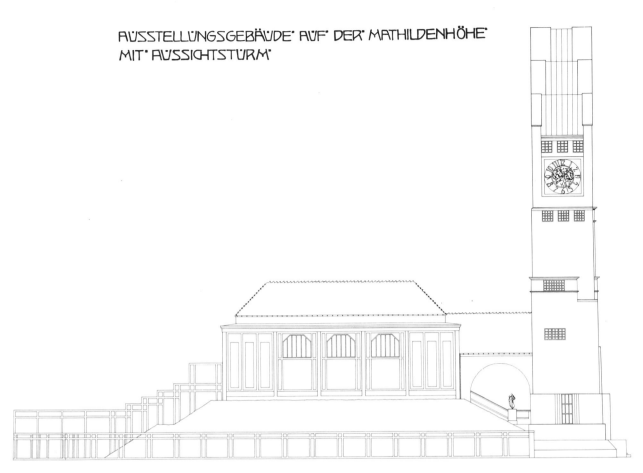

AUSSTELLUNGSGEBÄUDE· AUF· DER· MATHILDENHÖHE·
MIT· AUSSICHTSTURM·

Exhibition Building and Wedding Tower,
west elevation (from the original drawing).

of the surfaces. The lightly coffered 2.20 metre high socle is grey chisel-hammered concrete, then all the surfaces above it are painted white. The floor of the hall, with its irregular tiles, is handled in the same manner as the room socle.'

'At the entrance to the exhibition halls proper it seems important to explain the basic idea on which the whole design was based. Generally the whole building should be an exhibition building, not just a covering for works of art and the applied arts. It should also allow for all types of exhibition, whether they originate from local or individual interest. The building should be a setting for all types of gathering, whether they are called to listen to a talk on arts and crafts or accounts of travels. Further demands are to be fulfilled, demands required in a building with such a wide acceptance of artists' works and music. The range of subjects developing from the public interest is endless, so the space must be versatile to be of general use.'

'The room dimensions which have been conceived on a universal basis will correspond with all emotions and their effect on the realm of beauty and the field of technology, with everything new from the vast range of craft design, and with all values from the great variety of intellectual work. They consist of three parts arranged together on the reservoir, each as an independent entity. Each hall has its own entrance, all the halls can be inter-connected and all are provided with exits to the rose-garden. In addition to exhibitions which use all the halls because of the abundance of works, there are others needing only one hall. Three different exhibitions could be made open to the general public at the same time. The scheme shown in the drawings is in accordance with the requirements for varied use. The building becomes a machine!'

'Up to a height of 3.30 metres the walls contain a lay-out of equally spaced timber dowels, in order to be able to take fixings of all types in arbitrary places on the hall walls. The floor is "Riemenboden" that is easy to replace.'

ALTERNATIV·PROJECT·FÜR·DEN·AVSSICHTSTHVRM.

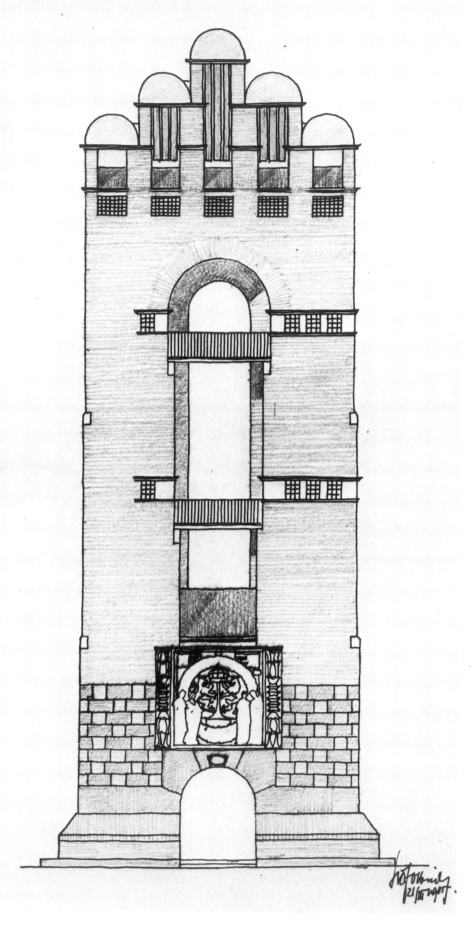

Sketch for an observation tower on the Mathildenhöhe, 1900.

Left
Preliminary drawing for the Wedding Tower, dated March 1905.

Opposite
The Wedding Tower and Exhibition Building viewed from the east.

Page 106
The Wedding Tower, Exhibition Building and Russian Chapel, and *(below)* entrance pavilion of the Exhibition Building.

Page 107
Detail of the Wedding Tower gable and view of the Exhibition Building from the Tower forecourt.

Plan of the Mathildenhöhe with the
Exhibition Building complex (from the
original drawing).

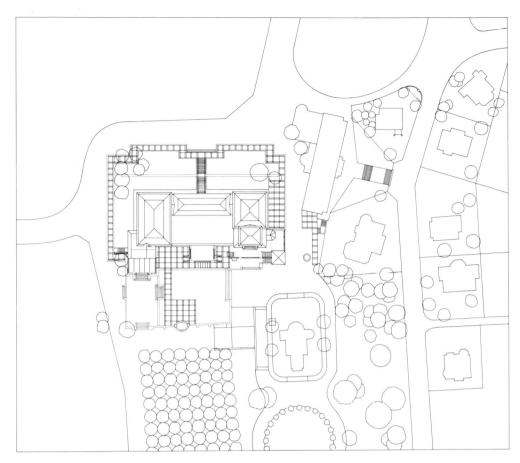

Opposite
The Exhibition Building viewed from the
Wedding Tower.

'So as not to dictate a decorative theme for the changing exhibition settings from
the beginning, the structural part of the hall will be shown as such undisguised. It
seems likely that the building and its surroundings will be used exclusively for
summer exhibitions. The citizens of the town will share the special enjoyment
with the arriving foreign guests between the months of May and the beginning of
November — a time when Darmstadt and its surroundings display an abundance
of beautiful natural scenery, and when the gardens and houses provide the
loveliest scenes. This great merit of having the city so closely bound with nature
assumes a natural vigour, from which arises the conviction that such a
pronounced character should be developed, combining the winter's peace with
the annual summery citizens' Festival of the Fruit. From such a beginning an
event for both town and country can arise.'

'All of these feelings, as previously mentioned, were determining factors for the
building. Between the two lateral top-lit halls, together 537 square metres of floor
space, is the connected side-lit hall on the west side of the building complex, with
a width of 8.70 metres and a length of 29 metres (251.4 square metres). Largely
planned for the presentation of entire room lay-outs, this hall can easily be
divided into a number of smaller rooms. The open space on the high reservoir
terrace, bordered on the north, east and west by the hall building, will be utilised
for horticultural exhibitions. Through the gaps left by the large garden wall, with
vines and roses on its inner side, it is possible to enjoy the view of the beauty of
the monument site and the tower forecourt, to sense the peace of the
Platanenhain and see the silhouette of the town. So this high garden enclosed by
quiet walls is a fitting place for the display of works of sculpture in the open air.'

'The land to the east of the building, bordered by pergolas and reached by a
staircase leading from the side-lit hall, is also planned for garden art, and part can
be specially devoted to churchyard art. The enclosing elements for the spot are
basically the long, blank building wall on the high area, the rose-covered slope,
the end leaf-wall of the pergolas and the existing birch stock, forming an effective
area for the memorial of harmony, the cult of the flower. The whole building is
constructed in reinforced concrete. All the halls are designed to be safe in fire.

Exhibition buildings, rear view.

Timber roofs are only used where they are completely closed off from the rooms by a ceiling. The value of this facility will be reflected in the insurance premium figures. As all exhibitions will take place during the summer months no basic heating or lighting installations have been planned. Further, the existing foundations of the high reservoir but not the vaulted chamber cover are supported directly and regularly through the concrete covering. This very simple and argument free construction technique serves as an exercise with the execution of this building, and its solution will have a marked effect on the further development of exhibition building. The nature of this concrete construction has other formal results on the viewed side which correspond to the appearance of the plans. The choice of this construction system to me lies in the possible radical performance of the material, which will effect the whole range of architectural ideas.'

'At the north-west corner of the exhibition building the mass of the Wedding Tower rises up from the green site formed by the leafy canopy of the plane tree grove and the vine-covered pergola. A connecting building establishes a passage between the grey mass of the exhibition house and that of the tower. This in turn consists of a broad substructure, a soaring tower shaft and a five-pinnacled crown. From the tower forecourt, eleven steps lead up towards the vaulted tower hall. This is closed off from the outside by a wrought-iron gate bearing the city arms in bronze in the centre. In the middle section of the tower the open staircase, covered by the roof of the connecting building, leads to the large exhibition hall. The tower staircase first links the tower Halle with rooms used for security and sanitary purposes. Up above this there is the first observation stage with a high barrel-vaulted roof. Fresco paintings on the walls and on the vault relate the life-story of the Grand Duke up to his wedding day.'

Great Hall of the Exhibition Building.

'Further on the steps lead to the second observation room. The walls are hung with embroidered works recording events from the life of the Grand Duchess up until February 2nd, 1905. Decoration such as tapestries are suggested and considered as donations. Beyond the clock mechanism one reaches the upper viewing hall. Pictures on panels between the windows tell the history of Darmstadt up to the completion of the building. A spiral staircase leads from here up to the chapel in the tower crown which, however, will not be open to the public. The windows of the rooms situated at different heights necessarily effect the appearance of the facade; they will be combined in groups and particularly stressed by stone frames. Above the entrance doorway the votive relief of stone is set into the dark brickwork.'

'In front of a myrtle wreath that encircles the arms of Brabant and Lich and above which the whole giant tablet is positioned, stands on the left the armour-clad standard-bearer of Hesse, who defends Art, and on the right an armed knight who escorts Beauty. The huge composed mass of the tower will be constructed in dark-red bricks and above this the black-violet pillars of the pinnacles will reach up to a greater height to complete the whole edifice in gentle curves. In the chapel niches thus formed, bronze chimes specially provided from donations will be hung, and their striking mechanism will be connected with the clock in the tower. The vertical mass of the Wedding Tower together with the horizontally arranged mass of the exhibition building will establish a monumental unity that will stand out as a landmark in the townscape. Seen from afar, as well as close up, they will inspire a dutiful reverance: Be silent, give eternal tidings from the passion of citizens at the time of a most joyful, happy celebration of life!' *(Darmstädter Tagblatt, 7/8.3.1906.)*

OPEL WORKER'S HOUSE

A major section of the Darmstadt Artists' Colony Exhibition of 1908 (Hessische Landesausstellung für freie und angewandte Kunst) was devoted to the 'Klein-Wohnungs-Kolonie' (Small House Colony) set in a small cul-de-sac in the eastern corner of the Mathildenhöhe. The colony represented a positive attempt to tackle the problems of providing cheap, well-designed housing for the lower and middle classes, and consisted of six houses, two two-family houses, a double house for two families and three one-family houses, each designed by a different architect.

Olbrich was responsible for the 'Arbeiterhaus Opel' (Opel Worker's House), which was sponsored by the automobile manufacturer Wilhelm Open of Rüsselsheim. 'The built cost of the house on a site (in Rüsselsheim) is at most 4,000M, the cost of construction and furniture is included in the house. The house is built throughout in quarry stone and brick by the firm J. Wagner . . . The roof is covered with plain tiles and the external walls are rendered. The oven and the stove are supplied by the firm Karl Thomann, Offenbach a.M. The furniture was made by the firm Schöndorff Brothers of Düsseldorf. The landscape work was carried out by the Grossgärtnerei Henkel.' *(Illustrierter Katalog der Hessischen Landesausstellung für freie und angewandte Kunst* Darmstadt 1908, p.91.)

The ground floor of the Arbeiterhaus Opel consisted of a large multi-purpose room — lit by two large opposing window bays — and a small kitchen area. A spiral staircase immediately to the right of the entrance led up to two twin bedrooms and a toilet. The rooms were simple yet bright and cheerfully decorated. The living area, with its exposed rafters and abstract flower frieze, was subdivided into areas for dining, relaxation and working.

Arbeiterhaus Opel: view from the south-west and basement, ground and first floor plans (from the original drawings).

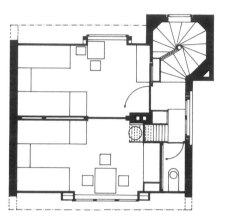

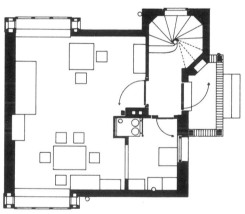

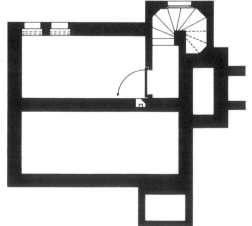

ARBEITERWOHNHAVS ·· FVR ·EINE· FAMILIE·

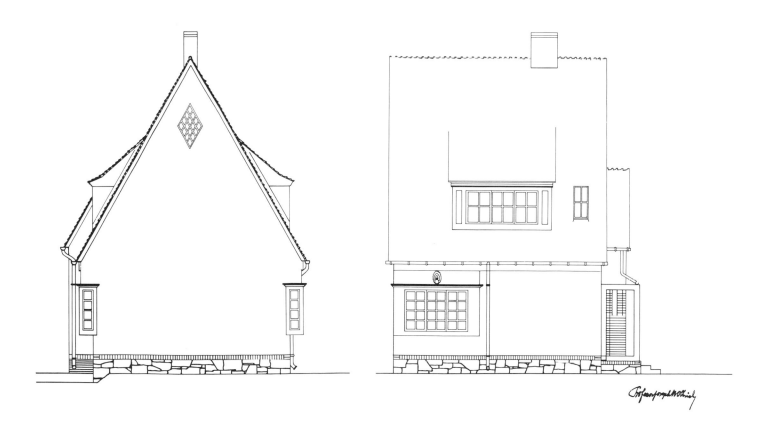

South, east, north and west elevations (from
the original drawings).

Opposite and right
Opposing corners of the ground floor living-area, complete with a portrait of Grand Duke Ernst Ludwig.

First floor bedrooms.

Project for the remodelling of an Opel car, 1906 (from the original drawing).

115

OBERHESSISCHES HAUS

The desire to provide a major display of Oberhesse (Upper Hesse) crafts at the 1908 Exhibition, prompted by the success of the Hessische Zimmer at the 1902 Turin Exhibition, led to the formation in the summer of 1907 of a twenty-five member 'Gesellschaft für Errichtung eines Oberhessischen-Ausstellungshauses zu Darmstadt GmbH' (Committee for the erection of an Upper Hesse Exhibition House in Darmstadt). The 'Oberhessisches Haus' was to be designed by Olbrich on a site directly to the east of the Ernst Ludwig Haus.

'For the exterior architecture, the smooth form and surface effect of the heavy, monumental composition with the far-extended porch betraying Meister Olbrich's individuality, the artist, in the given building material of light-grey basalt [Oberhessische Basaltlava] with its natural light-reddish undertones which make the grey colour seem extremely attractive and warm, has come across an extremely effective and efficient building material with a character which he has taken into account with fine artistic understanding. The commendable attempt to provide as much air and light as possible for the house and its occupants is noticeable even in the exterior of the fine building with its numerous delightful terraces, verandas and balconies on all floors, and certainly a primary determining factor in their construction was also the marvellous panoramas and views over the surrounding natural scenery. And a bright, light and airy clearly-arranged room lay-out also dominates the interior of the building, the supporting element of which is an extraordinarily attractively designed and executed Halle, which reaches through two storeys and around which the room suites are grouped . . . Professor Jos. M. Olbrich controlled the interior arrangements in every respect. The artist has designed not only the impressive Musiksalon, artistically conceived down to the smallest detail with light mahogany carved and gilded decoration, worked inlays and splendid casements, but also the comfortably habitable Herrenzimmer [study] in light, natural oak with the characteristic fascinating surface effect of the furniture, and the large calm and friendly Speisezimmer [dining-room] with its thick walnut furniture in a brown tortoise-shell colour and heavily carved wall-panelling. The Speisezimmer with its fine large projecting terrace and full height windows is almost an ideal room.' (Darmstädter Tagblatt, 28.7.1908.)

The Oberhessisches Haus was purchased after the 1908 Exhibition (which ran from May 23rd until October 31st) by the Ofenfabrikanten Roeder, since when the house has been internally subdivided and the exterior modified.

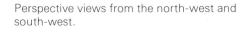

Perspective views from the north-west and south-west.

Detail of the south-west corner with garden loggia.

Right
The music-room and dining-room.

Below
Ground and first floor plans (from the original drawings).

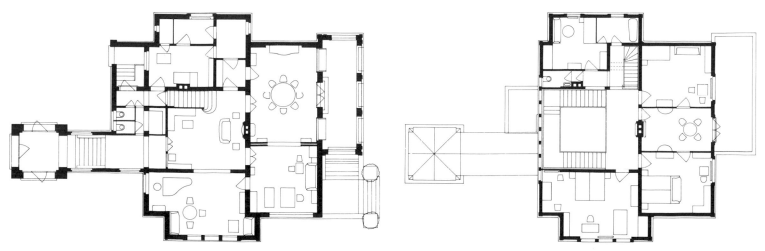

GLÜCKERT HAUS REDECORATIONS

Julius Glückert commissioned Olbrich to alter and redecorate parts of his Grosses Glückert Haus for the 1908 Exhibition. Extensions were planned but the only changes that were eventually made were to the interiors on the ground floor, notably the Halle, the Speisezimmer, the Herrenzimmer and the Damenzimmer. Described in the *Darmstädter Zeitung* (1.9.1908) as 'the best, finest, most intimate and well-devised work of the late master', the redecorated Halle was dismantled in 1965 and replaced with a replica of the 1901 decoration without realising that the exisiting work was by Olbrich.

Staircase and gallery in the redecorated Halle, and *(below)* same view showing original condition of the Halle in 1901.

Opposite
Fireplace bay of the redecorated Halle, showing the dining-room beyond.

OTHER WORK IN GERMANY
MISCELLANEOUS PROJECTS 1899-1908

Whilst he was working on plans for the major 1901 Colony Exhibition, Olbrich was offered a number of local commissions. Gustav Römheld, leader of the Grand Duke's Cabinet and a potent force behind the establishment and financial organisation of the Artists' Colony, lived at Alexandraweg 14 and between 1899 and 1900 Olbrich redecorated the central rooms of his house.

In the spring of 1900 Olbrich designed a group of houses, also on the Alexandraweg (nos. 3-7, destroyed in 1944), for the Darmstadt building contractor Wilhelm Ganss. The three houses shared a symmetrical street facade and various details, including the distinctive curved gables and the plaster foliage decoration, reveal similarities with Olbrich's contemporary colony houses, particularly the Grosses Glückert Haus.

An unexecuted project by Olbrich for the Harres Häusergruppe (Harres House Group) on the Thurmstrasse in Darmstadt dates from 1901. Again Olbrich used familiar elements: the checked pattern of tiles as on his own house, the semicircular and lattice windows of the Kleines Glückert Haus and the distinctive colony garden gates. He has attempted to provide an individual identity for each separate home; a concept that was to be developed further with the Dreihäusergruppe of the 1904 Exhibition.

Yet another scheme designed by Olbrich in the vicinity of the Artists' Colony in Darmstadt was the Doppelhaus Stade (Stade Double House) in Prinz-Christians-Weg (formerly Victoria-Melita-Weg 19-21) erected between 1901 and 1902 and destroyed in 1944. The large semi-detached house was commissioned by the brothers Gustav and Joseph Stade. Located directly on the colony axis below the Ernst Ludwig Haus, opposite the site that had been occupied by the temporary Exhibition Gallery, the Doppelhaus Stade loosely resembled Olbrich's unbuilt project for the Harres Häusergruppe.

In Kronberg im Taunus, a small town to the north-west of Frankfurt, Olbrich designed a house for Albert Hochstrasser, with drawings dating from the summer of the 1901 Exhibition. The house was an attractive composition that followed the development of the Colony houses in its sparse yet subtle use of decoration; the checkered pattern that wrapped around the ground floor, for instance, was repeated on a smaller scale in a band running under the roof eaves. The west facade reveals Olbrich's characteristic treatment of juxtaposing symmetrical and asymmetrical features; in this case, the central window grid arrangement against the entrance porch and the small curved gable above. Furthermore the porch and gable themselves appear asymmetrical by the positioning of the entrance steps and a small window. Olbrich even symbolised Hochstrasser's interest in gardening by the use of flower motifs in the decoration of the house. The Hochstrasser house and its outbuildings still exist today (Schönberger Feld 9), though in a slightly modified form.

Salon and living-room for Gustav Römheld.

Opposite above
Harres Häusergruppe project, 1901, designed for a site on the Thurmstrasse in Darmstadt.

Opposite below
Doppelhaus Stade, 1901-02, perspective from the north-west.

Page 122 above
The Grand Duke's apartment in the Alten Schloss in Giessen, living-room, 1906.

Page 122 below
Villa Kuntze, dining-room, 1902.

Page 123
Design for a wall-mounted gas lamp, front and side elevation, 1901.

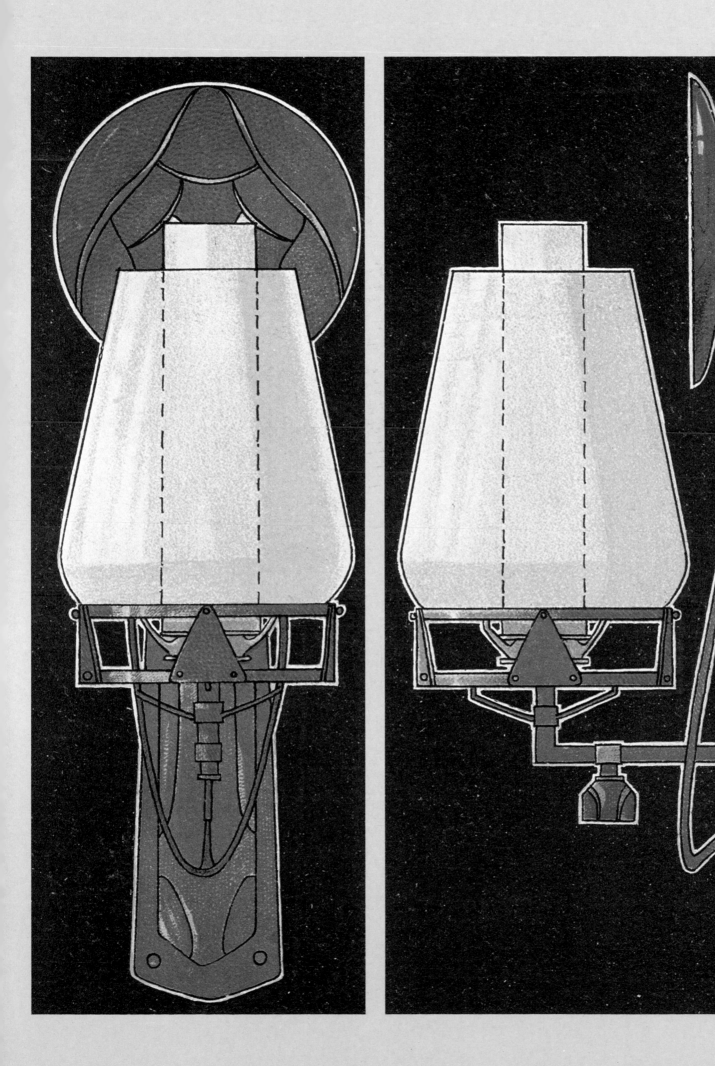

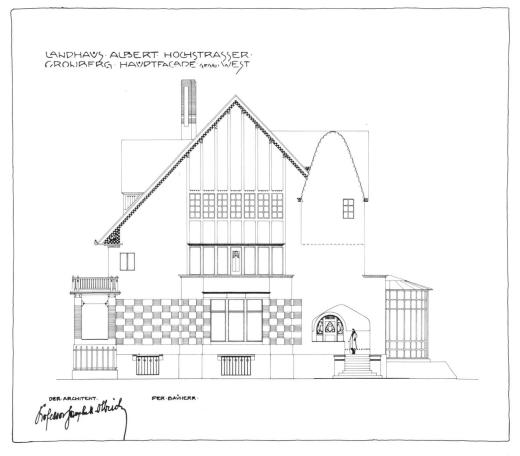

Top
Ganss house group, 1900, contemporary photograph.

Above
Sarre house project, 1903, perspective drawing.

Above right
Villa Kuntze, Berlin, 1902, perspective drawing.

Right
Hochstrasser house, 1901, west elevation (from the original drawing).

Opposite above
Writing desk and cigar cabinet designed for the firm of Josef Trier, 1902.

Opposite below left
Watercolour sketch for a music cabinet, c. 1902.

Opposite below right
Design for a clock, 1902.

Olbrich's first German commission far from Darmstadt was for a house for Carl Kuntze in Berlin, built in 1902 on a large site between the Steglitzer Damm, Halskestrasse and Albrechtstrasse. The Villa Kuntze was a sizeable three-storey house with a basement, centred around a double height Halle; the elevations were kept fairly simple by grouping the windows in panels separated from the plastered wall surfaces. In 1910 the site was divided up and the villa was

125

subsequently surrounded by an estate of houses, the Albrechtspark, designed by Buchholz. Very little of the house remains today.

Olbrich's unexecuted project of 1903 for a house for Professor Friedrich Sarre, the art historian, was probably taken over from another architect. The small house was most likely intended for a site in Neubabelsberg.

In the ground of the Grand Duke's summer residence at Wolfsgarten bei Langen, between Darmstadt and Frankfurt, Olbrich built a small playhouse for the young Princess Elisabeth von Hessen, Ernst Ludwig's daughter from his first marriage, who later died in Petersburg of typhus at the age of seven. Erected in 1902, the house consisted of a covered porch and two small fully furnished rooms, with everything carefully scaled down to the size of the young child. Olbrich's increasing use of Biedermeier and Zopfstil (neo-Rococo) details at the expense of Jugendstil motifs is well illustrated in the overall appearance of the scheme. He nevertheless manages to introduce a few details of his own invention, including the 'pierced' chimney shaft, which repeats the oval wreath on the gable (with the initial 'E'), and the crown of open metalwork rising above the roof ridge. In addition Olbrich designed a special book of the fairy-tale *Es war einmal* ('Once upon a time') by Lise Ramspek for presentation to the Princess. The playhouse and its interiors remain in the possession of the present Grand Duke and are in very good condition.

In the summer of 1902, following the completion of the playhouse, the Grand Duke asked Olbrich to redecorate the Musiksaal (music hall) of the Neue Palais in Darmstadt. The 7 metre square room was lavishly decorated and furnished, but was destroyed along with the rest of the palace during the war.

Four years later Olbrich designed the Grand Duke's apartment in the Altes Schloss in Giessen, as part of the restoration scheme for the castle that had been started in 1893 under Ludwig Hoffmann.

The changing emphasis of Olbrich's work was not unnoticed at the First International Exhibition of Modern Decorative Art in Turin held in 1902: 'The design artist Prof. J. M. Olbrich appears to be endeavouring to free himself from certain extravagances and to find a simpler form-language, whereby his versatile talents have a more distinctly beneficial effect.' *(Deutsche Kunst und Dekoration* XI, p.72.) As the official delegate for Hesse Olbrich was responsible for a series of three interiors. The 'Hessische Zimmer' or 'Blaues Zimmer', a living-room in blue, grey and white, acted as a showcase for examples of the work of Hesse's craftsmen. The 'Schlafzimmer' and 'Teesalon', with furniture by the Glückert firm, attracted attention particularly for their colour schemes. For the 'Hessische Zimmer' Olbrich was awarded the first prize of 8,000 Francs.

Olbrich's contribution prompted an enthusiastic response from the critic for *The Studio:* 'German designers of decoration are just now divided into two parties, those who follow Olbrich and those who think there is no one like Behrens; but although these two artists of Darmstadt are rivals, their work is really not unlike. In Germany Behrens is considered the modern German master par excellence, but this is a mistake. His style, it is true, is thoroughly Viennese, with some of the Viennese imagination left out; but it is Olbrich who is the real leader, the real impersonation of modern tendencies, and whatever individual opinion may be as to his art as a whole, he is the very prince of modern decorators, the most powerful and prolific of them all.' *(The Studio* 27, 1903, p.190.)

Olbrich was not, however, accorded such praise from Alexander Koch, the Darmstadt publisher and art critic. Koch's large catalogue, which included about 500 photographs of the Turin exhibits, did not illustrate a single item by Olbrich, despite his success at the exhibition. From 1902 onwards Olbrich received little attention in Koch's journals, although the work of the other Colony members was well covered.

Playhouse built for Princess Elisabeth von Hessen at Wolfsgarten, 1902 (from the original drawings).

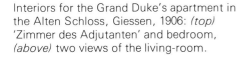
Interiors for the Grand Duke's apartment in the Alten Schloss, Giessen, 1906: *(top)* 'Zimmer des Adjutanten' and bedroom, *(above)* two views of the living-room.

Probably as a direct result of his 1902 exhibits, Olbrich was commissioned in the following year to design a 'Herrenzimmer' (study) for the Turin home of the engineer Carlo Stratta, though the plans were never carried out.

Hermann Muthesius (1861-1927), the enthusiastic supporter of contemporary English architecture who was largely responsible for introducing the ideas of the Domestic Revival to Germany, described Olbrich's contribution to the Louisiana Purchase International Exposition held in St. Louis in 1904 in *Deutsche Kunst und Dekoration*: 'Among the German interior artists at the St. Louis Exhibition Olbrich takes first place. He has shown six rooms, together designed as a ''Sommersitz eines Kunstfreundes'' [Summer Residence of an Art-lover], arranged as a group of buildings and enclosing a delightful decorated court with water pools and landscaping. The fact that Olbrich is a brilliant decorator was clear from the beginning. Here he shows that he is an inspired interior-architect in the best sense of the word. The work seems to be dashed off with the greatest of ease. Each of the rooms has its own special character and each is full of original ideas . . .'

'The whole exhibit is a masterful achievement. It speaks in an agreeable, light and

Fountain court, 1904 St Louis Exhibition, perspective (from the original drawing).

stylish way, not only to the expert but also to the general public, and for an exhibition that is a great advantage. This whole Olbrich-Art has something ingratiating, soft, feminine. It is specifically Viennese. It seems like a beautiful girl who wins all hearts with her charm, without needing to express sincere profound thoughts. It stands thereby at a great distance from the heavier, thick-blooded German works that almost all take on a rather philosophical meaning, that one is more or less compelled to puzzle out in order to understand them fully.' (Hermann Muthesius, *Deutsche Kunst und Dekoration* XV, p.210.)

These 'heavier' German buildings at St. Louis included Bruno Möhring's exhibition hall and a reconstruction of part of the Charlottenburg Castle. Olbrich's 1,500 square metre 'Sommersitz' was located between two existing buildings and was to house the applied arts exhibits of the south-west German States of Hesse, Baden, Württemberg and Elsass-Lothringen. The design dates from spring 1903 and consisted of twelve rooms arranged symmetrically around the fountain court; Olbrich was also responsible for the internal arrangement of six of the rooms: the 'Wohnzimmer' (living-room), the 'Teesalon' (tea salon), the 'Bibliothek' (library), the 'Speisezimmer' (dining-room), the 'Musikzimmer' (music-room) and the 'Herrenzimmer' (study).

Study for Carlo Stratta (unexecuted), fireplace elevation (from the original drawing).

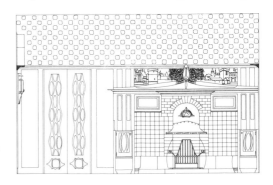

The design was seen very much as a backcloth for the exhibits and, from a very early stage, Olbrich collaborated with his fellow participants from Darmstadt, Mainz and Worms. The fountain court was painted white and had deep-red tiled roofs, contrasting with the blue water pools and green grass.

'The Olbrich pavilion was opened with enormous success. It was described as the jewel of the whole . . . by the leader of the American art section.' *(Möbel und Dekoration* 7, 1904.)* Olbrich was awarded the Grand Prix and a Gold Medal;

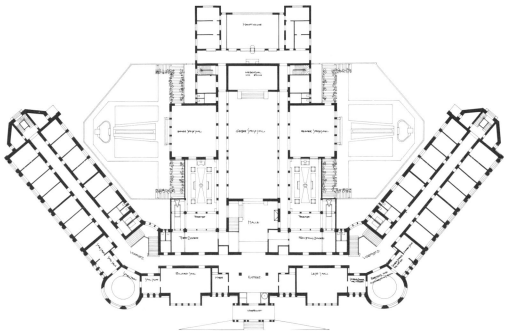

Hotel Königswart project, 1902: preliminary studies, and facade and ground floor plan (from the original drawing).

apparently Frank Lloyd Wright sent some of his assistants to see the exhibit. In January 1905, Olbrich was given corresponding membership of the American Institute of Architects.

Perhaps the most bizarre manifestation of Olbrich's skills was revealed in his project of 1902 for a large spa-hotel at Königswart in Böhmen for the Prince of Metternich. Three years earlier, while Olbrich was still in Vienna, he had designed an interior scheme for the 'Gastzimmer' (guest room) of the Prince's Villa Metternich. The hotel scheme was to be financed by an Anglo-Austrian company together with the Prince, and Olbrich was to have been responsible for all design aspects of the scheme. What would have been his most ambitious building to date was, however, destined to remain unrealised.

The room arrangement was typical of the many grand hotels of the period, catering for the social élite who visited the spa resorts and governed by their strict etiquette. About 400 bedrooms were placed in a long four-storey block with central corridors and this was articulated into three sections, half enclosing the ground floor halls and service rooms. The two junction points were emphasised by circular turret-like structures which contained galleried communal rooms. The staircases were also located at these points, as well as at the ends of the extended wings. The exterior of the Königswart Hotel project displayed a whole range of historical and geographical motifs, and was to be executed in an extensive variety of materials and colours. The central section of the front elevation was marked by three curved gables, used previously in the Hochstrasser house and to become an increasingly common feature of Olbrich's designs. In 1904-05 Olbrich began a project for another hotel, the Eleonorenhotel, which was to be built in the grounds of the Alte Palais in Darmstadt, but this too remained unexecuted.

A major exhibition of German art to be held in Cologne in 1905 was planned by the members of the 'Verband der Kunstfreunde in den Ländern am Rhein' (Association of Art-lovers in the States on the Rhine), founded in May 1904. 'The assigned site on the Rhine, the so-called Kaisergarten, was covered with trees but otherwise vacant; it had to be uniformly set out to an artistic plan. Six architects from the Verband — Peter Behrens, Düsseldorf; Franz Brantzky, Cologne; J. M. Olbrich, Darmstadt; Hermann Billing and Friedrich Ratzel, Karlsruhe and Theodor Fischer, Stuttgart — were invited to make proposals, and from them Hermann Billing received the prize. Unfortunately difficulties arose in the negotiations for the Kaisergarten; the sale of exchequer to the city could not be managed; so as not to rush into the choice of a new site, in November 1904 the adjournment was given for the exhibition from 1905 to 1906.' *(Deutsche Kunstausstellung, Köln 1906, Jahresgabe des Verbandes der Kunstfreunde in den Ländern am Rhein 1906,* p.1.)

As the new site in the Floragarten (Botanical Garden), to the north of the Kaisergarten, was rather different in character, set further back from the Rhine and with an existing restaurant and gardens, a new series of plans was drawn up. The central exhibition building was designed by Hermann Billing and Bernhard Pankok, Olbrich designed the 'Frauenrosenhof' and Peter Behrens the 'Tonhaus'. 'The man from Vienna, in whose art the proximity of oriental splendour was reflected, has acclimatised himself noticeably. In red sandstone he built himself an interim cloistered court, full of a mediaeval Romanesque feeling, in order to exhibit his fashionable, truly Viennese jewellery; a strange contrast which clearly illustrates our cultural indecision.' (Ruldolf Klein, *Deutsche Kunst und Dekoration* XVIII, p.636.)

The Frauenrosenhof served as an exhibition hall for expensive hand-made items, mostly designed by Olbrich himself for rich women clients of Cologne. The building was sited at the edge of a lake, its enveloping walls and arched arcade producing an unusually intimate effect. The Frauenrosenhof still exists, with drastic modifications, in the Cologne Flora Park adjacent to the Zoo.

Joseph Olbrich had designed buildings for his home town of Troppau in 1891, when as a student he entered a competition for a museum, and in 1898 when he planned the Café Niedermeyer, but neither of these projects had come to fruition. In 1904, however, he was able to design and build a house for his younger brother Edmund, at Ratiborer Strasse 17, next door to the house where the brothers had been born and raised. Edmund had inherited the family confectionery business, and the new building contained his shop premises on the ground floor and his own rooms on the upper levels. The street facade consisted of articulated brickwork on the ground and first floors, with all the windows and doors placed within a regular grid of vertical panels. The bold curved gable above was plastered and its height was exaggerated by an oval decorative panel linked to the tall attic window. This oval motif was repeated at ground level in the two small basement windows and again in the decorative panels over the doors which included the initials of the two brothers.

Olbrich was among the 184 entrants for the competition held in 1906-7 for the design of a number of water towers for the city of Hamburg. In January of 1907 the projects were assessed and prizes were awarded to Karl Storck, Dr Vetterlein (both from Darmstadt), Hans Poelzig and Bodo von Ebhardt. Olbrich submitted schemes for three of the proposed sites, but none was among the winning entries.

To mark the 300th Jubilee of the city of Mannheim in 1907, a major exhibition of art and applied art was held. The central hall, the Kunsthalle, was designed by Hermann Billing, and within it Olbrich was responsible for the Galerieraum

The Frauenrosenhof in Cologne's Flora Park, 1906 (altered).

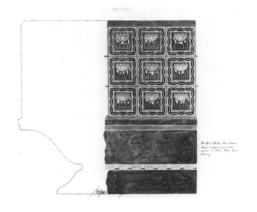

BLVMENTOPF·ENTW.PROF.J·M·OLBRICH·DARMSTADT·1905·

Flower vase designed for Villeroy and Boch, 1905.

FRVHSTVCKSERVICE·ENTW·PROF·JOS·M·OLBRICH FVR·FRAV·HORTENSE·VON·GVILLAVME·KÖLN·

TEEKANNE

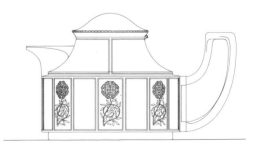

Teapot design for the 1906 Cologne Exhibition (from the original drawing).

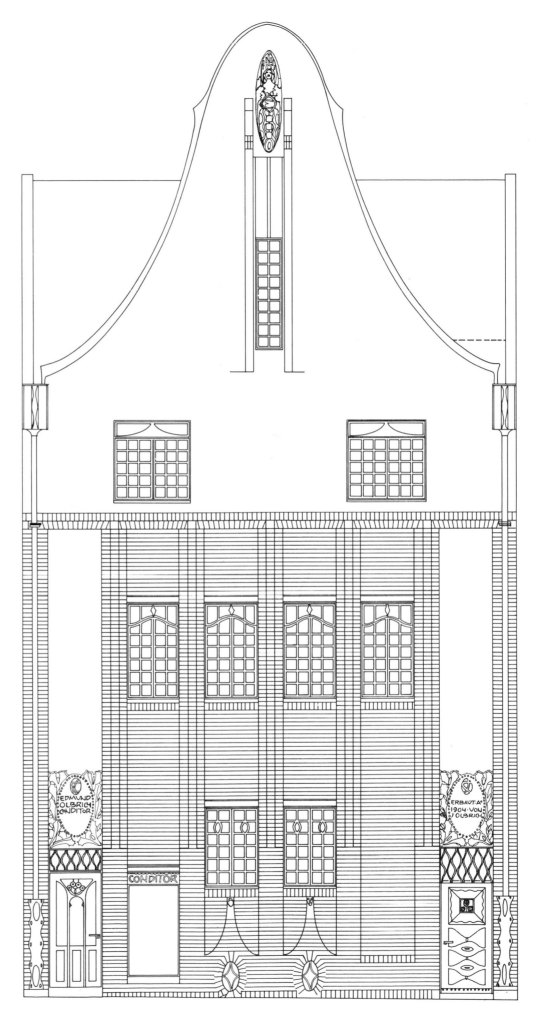

Edmund Olbrich house, Troppau, 1904,
facade (from the original drawing).

Three designs for the Hamburg water tower competition, 1907.

(gallery room), the Gemäldesaal für ein vornehmes Privathaus (painting hall for an elegant private house) and the Damensalon (ladies' room). 'Also in the previous year, at the Mannheim Exhibition, his interior art surpassed everything executed by the German competitors.' (Ludwig Hevesi, *Altkunst-Neukunst Wien 1894-1908,* Wien, 1909, p.325.)

In the same year the Committee zur gärtnerischen Verschönerung des Luisenplatzes (Committee for the landscaping improvements of the Luisenplatz) asked Olbrich to make suggestions for Darmstadt's central square. This included the erection of two fountains, which were paid for from the takings of the 1905 Gartenbau Ausstellung (Horticultural Exhibition). The built scheme differed slightly from Olbrich's drawings, and today, despite the recent modifications to the square, one of the fountains still remains.

Olbrich's entry for the 'Wettbewerb zur Gewinnung von Entwürfen für die Haupt- und Seitenfassaden des neuen Bahnhofsgebäudes der schweizerischen Bundesbahn in Basel' (Competition for the preparation of designs for the main

Above and below
Gallery and 'Damensalon' at the 1907
Mannheim Jubilee Exhibition.

Right
Luisenplatz fountains, Darmstadt, 1907,
contemporary photograph and section (from
the original drawing).

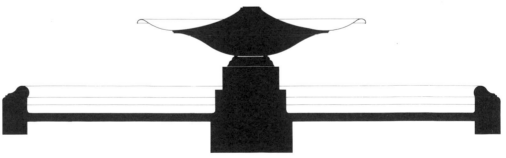

and side facades of the new station building of the Swiss Bundesbahn in Basel),
held in 1903, received the third prize of 3,000 Francs (no first prize was given), and
proved influential on subsequent station design in Germany. The competition
was restricted to forty-five entrants and their schemes were displayed in the
Basel Gewerbemuseum from July 2nd to July 5th. The jury said of Olbrich's
design: 'The essential merit of this project lies in the use of suspended and
cantilevered beams [Gelenkträgern] which span freely across the whole of the
entrance hall, so any intermediate supports that would hinder such a building for
rail transport can be avoided . . . The architectural design aims for the most
practical simplification of the technical arrangement and a direct connection to
the construction system and therefore for the elimination of all details that have
only a traditional aesthetic value.' *(Schweizerische Bauzeitung.)*

Four years later a similar competition was held for the design of Darmstadt station, open to any architects resident in Germany, which the Grand Duke stipulated was to be by a 'modern' rather than by a 'style-architect'. Seventy-five entries were exhibited at the Alte Schloss in Darmstadt from February 27th to March 11th, 1907. Prizes were awarded to Professor Pützer of Darmstadt and Professor Klingholz of Aachen (1st), Joseph Olbrich (2nd) and Bonatz, Martin and Taut of Stuttgart and Brurein of Berlin. Pützer's scheme was finally built, with some modifications, and exists to this day.

In 1907-08 Olbrich designed a small house with a studio for his painter friend Max Clarenbach in the small town of Wittlaer, north of Düsseldorf (Duisburger Strasse 15a). The simple, unpretentious building, distinguished by its mansard

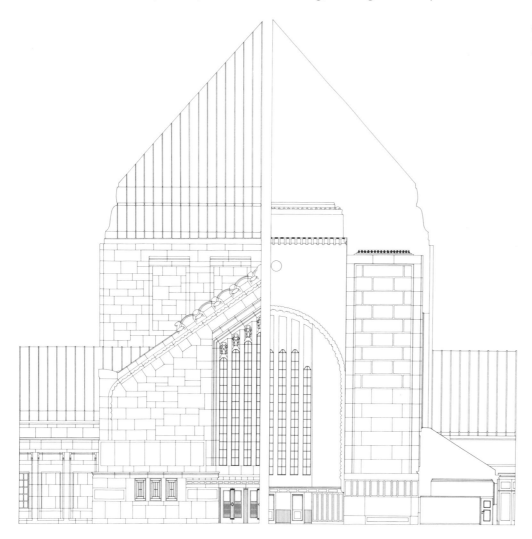

Combined elevation and section of the Main Hall of Darmstadt Station project, 1907, and front elevation of Basel Station project, 1903.

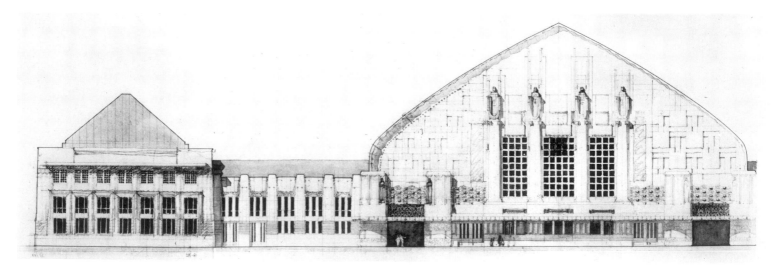

roof and a projecting bay overlooking the Rhine's flood plain, still exists today in a slightly modified form.

Whilst work was proceeding on the huge Warenhaus Tietz, Olbrich designed a number of large private houses around Cologne, all of which have since been destroyed.

Two adjacent houses built for Frau van Geleen and Hugo Kruska in Köln-Lindenthal and the Villa Banzhaf in Köln-Marienburg were designed by Olbrich and their completion arranged by his assistants. All three bore a close formal resemblance to the Oberhessisches Haus, with the characteristic mansard roof and classical loggia.

On a rather grander scale was the residence built in extensive grounds in Köln-Marienburg for Joseph Feinhals, the wealthy tobacco merchant. Olbrich claimed inspiration from the architects of the High Renaissance, including Bramante and Peruzzi, and this influence is very clear in the monumental, symmetrical house with its carefully balanced window arrangement and Doric colonnade facing the garden.

Haus Clarenbach, Wittlaer bei Düsseldorf, 1907-08, south side overlooking the Rhine.

Haus Geleen and Haus Kruska, Köln-Lindenthal, 1907-08, contemporary photograph.

Villa Banzhaf, Köln-Marienburg, 1908, contemporary photograph of entrance.

Above and right
Haus Feinhals, Köln-Marienburg, 1908:
entrance porch, view from entrance gate,
entrance and garden facades.

LOW COST HOUSING PROJECTS

Not until the turn of the century were the real problems of providing low-cost quality housing tackled by continental architects, by which time the ideas of the English Garden City movement had become firmly established. After the 1901 Darmstadt Artists' Colony Exhibition some criticism had been levelled at the extravagance and exclusive nature of the artists' homes; this was to a certain extent contrary to their aims, and over the next few years a number of moves were made to answer the critics.

From 1902 onwards Olbrich undertook a number of projects for low-cost housing, although the only plans that came to fruition were for the Dreihäusergruppe of 1904, which was only a 'one-off' project, and the Opel Arbeiterhaus of 1908.

Olbrich made drawings for a group of three single-family houses in 1902 probably intended for a site to the north-east of the Mathildenhöhe. The scheme was never carried out but the plans were exhibited at Giessen and Darmstadt in 1903. 'Also provoking particular interest are the cheaper houses, three in number for the time being, which are to be built, on the initiative of his Royal Highness the Grand Duke, commanding the highest part of the same site. Each of these buildings, thought of as comfortable and idyllic homes for the better-off middle class, will cost only 18,000 Marks including complete ground floor furnishings. On the ground floor they will contain a small hall, three rooms and a kitchen, on the upper floor three bedrooms, a bath and a small closet, and a maids' room in the roof storey. The plan of the three houses, in the middle of which is a court, is arranged in such a manner that no resident can overlook the entrance of another house from his own. Throughout the houses there is a feeling of pleasantness and appropriateness, and the whole layout is truly picturesque.' *(Darmstädter Zeitung,* 15.10.1903.) The essentially compact lay-out and simple construction would keep the cost of the houses low, and the curved gables would provide a distinctive character, following the similar gables Olbrich used in the Hochstrasser house and Königswart Hotel project. (He may well have 'borrowed' this feature from Baillie Scott's entry for the 'Haus eines Kunstfreundes' (House for an Art-lover) competition, which was held in 1901, and for which Olbrich was a judge.) The houses also have an almost total lack of applied ornament, the decorative effects being achieved by the variety and detailing of the building materials.

In 1906-07 Olbrich produced a major scheme for a Gartenvorstadt am Hohlen Weg (Garden Suburb on the Hohlen Weg) in Darmstadt, for the same site that had been selected for his 1902 project. With a knowledge of the English developments and the experience of the 1905 Gartenbau Exhibition and his earlier low-cost housing project, Olbrich aimed to produce an estate of new houses at a low cost which neither inhibited nor dictated to the individual occupants. 'Each plot will contain at least 500 square metres of which 19 × 20 metres will remain reserved for the garden. The house can be positioned on the site completely in accordance with the wishes of the owner. Building lines are not dictated unless they are in accordance with the character of the whole.' *(Darmstädter Tagblatt,* 12.6.1907.)

Initially sixteen houses were planned, to be built as show houses for the 1908 Colony Exhibition. Olbrich designed three different house types, of 2½, 2 and 1½ storeys at different prices. The latter scheme appears to be a forerunner of the Opel Arbeiterhaus. Although plans for the Gartenvorstadt were scheduled to go ahead in the summer of 1907, the scheme was abandoned and the Kleinwohnungskolonie was built for the 1908 Exhibition.

M. H. Baillie Scott: 'Dulce Domen', entry for the 'Haus eines Kunstfreundes' competition, 1901.

C. R. Mackintosh: 'Der Vogel', entry for the 'Haus eines Kunstfreundes' competition, 1901.

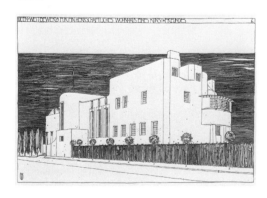

Project for a group of three single-family houses, Darmstadt, 1902: *(right)* perspective, *(below)* site plan, and *(bottom)* elevations (from the original drawings).

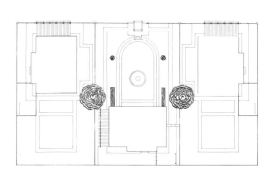

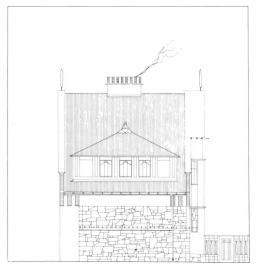

Three designs for the Hohlen Weg garden suburb project, Darmstadt, 1906-07: one and a half, two, and two and a half storey houses (elevations from the original drawings).

HAUS SILBER

At a Bayreuth Wagner concert Olbrich met the wife of Dr Erwin Angelo Silber, a doctor at the Stolzenberg Sanatorium. As a result in 1906 the couple asked him to design them a house in Bad Soden bei Salmünster, a small town to the north-east of Frankfurt. The house, at Marborner Strasse 6, is still in existence. Olbrich wrote to Mrs. Silber: 'Your requirements were rather extensive and it would be very difficult for me to be able to consider all the requests, especially with regard to the cost limit. The enclosed drawings have developed from the series of sketches and studies.'

'Position: I have placed the entrance to the house on the high-lying side of the sloping land and consequently retain the low-lying cleft for the very significant facade arrangement. The terrain falls in steps, which will be formed by banking. I mention principally the sloping land in the architectural context. Anything that consisted of verticals and horizontals would be distorted by the inclined ground surface. Therefore the sloping ground surface will be broken down into horizontal surfaces forming the garden terraces.'

Haus Silber, Bad Soden bei Salmünster, 1906, north, west, east and south elevations.

'With my visit to the site I shall make definite decisions.'

'Arrangement: The house path leads up to a covered forecourt. It is useful to have a protective roof over the front door in case of rain. The front door opens to the outside. Now one enters the white-striped hallway over four steps. Here coats and hats can be taken off, and if necessary the wash basin in the water closet can be used. To the right of the entrance, steps lead down to the kitchen rooms in the basement. The vestibule with the main staircase to the first floor is designed here as a spacious hall.'

'From the vestibule, in which there is a good place for your house-saint standing on the middle column of the inner fireproof partition, one is able to enter every room without having to pass through the other rooms. I also mention that the vestibule has white walls to harmonise with the brown woodwork of the stairs and doors. The house-saint can be placed against a gold background in a niche. The flowers which you place in front of it every day will create the atmosphere in the room with their bright colours!'

'The largest rooms — the children's room and the living/dining room — are placed on the main side of the house. The windows are so arranged that the walls will be useful for the arrangement of the furniture. A window can ruin everything. The living/dining room with its broad window can be beautifully arranged. Also the heaters are positioned so they do not get in the way, yet fulfill their function properly. A 2m 10cm wide opening which can be closed by glass doors leads into your room. The piano is best positioned in the corner so that, as a singer, you can project your voice into the room . . .'

'The children's room as well as the study offer the same advantages. In the latter in particular there is ample space for an extensive library. The corner in here will take a writing desk. From the position of the desk the eye can wander through the window to a view of the garden. I consider it essential — particularly for when guests are present — to place a water closet under the upper stair flight on the ground floor.'

'Then the bedrooms are arranged on the upper floor. Your brief has provided for so many rooms that I have had to divide the total and place half of them in the roof storey. It would be worth considering using the bedroom specified for your husband, because of its size, for the children's bedroom, then the smaller room can be reserved for your husband.'

'The air-bath is linked to the bathroom. In winter the air-bath can be shut by window panels. The bathroom is closed off from the air-bath by a glass wall. I will advise you totally against a deep round basin in the bathroom. It is simply impossible to make such basins watertight, and after a year's use a catastrophe often occurs. The rooms in the roof are allocated for future expansion and for guest rooms. In addition these rooms will function very effectively through the positioning of the windows. In the basement is the kitchen, the household cellar, then the washroom and a room that is absolutely essential for the household. This is for ironing, sewing, cleaning, storing preserved fruits etc. etc.'

'This very simple spirit, fixed by the plan, is also expressed on the facade. Everything indicates the inner life. Nothing will be masked or veiled. The facades are built from the inside out . . . The cost per square metre of the house is calculated at the cheapest as 175 Mk, so the building cost would be 24,325 Mk. In addition the payment for my work on the design, detail plans and detailed calculations would be 1,625 Mk, so the whole house will amount to 25,950 Mk.'

WARENHAUS TIETZ

Announce, oh noble building, for a long time to future generations
The genius and strength of the man, who created himself a memorial here:
Olbrich, your name lives on in this magnificent work,
You closed your eyes too soon to see it completed.

(Bronze memorial plaque, Warenhaus Tietz, now Kaufhof, Düsseldorf.)

Warenhaus Tietz, Düsseldorf, preliminary 1906 scheme and contemporary photograph of the Königsallee facade as built.

In autumn 1906 a competition, open to architects resident in Germany, was held for the design of a new department store for the firm of Leonhard Tietz in Düsseldorf. The site was in the city's main street, the Königsallee, and an appropriately imposing building was required. Two equal first prizes of 4,000 Marks were awarded to Rehberg and Lipp of Charlottenburg and Otto Engler of Düsseldorf, and two second prizes of 2,500 Marks were given to Joseph Olbrich and Otto and Paul Engler of Düsseldorf. A second round was then held between these four and also Wilhelm Kreis of Dresden. The jury was still unable to select an overall winning scheme, so three were chosen to be built in model form; those by Olbrich, Kreis and Engler. Finally Olbrich was awarded the commission.

Joseph Olbrich's individual involvement with the Warenhaus Tietz scheme was total. He completed nearly all of the drawings in his own hand and set up an office in Düsseldorf, where he spent an ever increasing amount of his time until his untimely death in August of 1908.

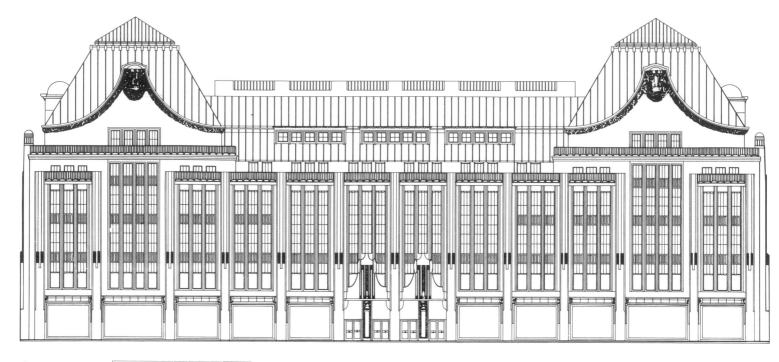

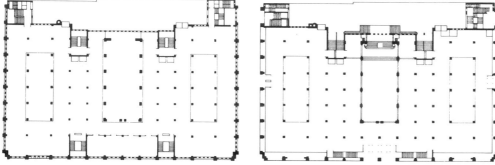

Entrance elevation, ground and upper floor plans (from the original drawings).

Olbrich described the seventeen metre high central light court as his 'Dom' (Cathedral). Indeed the high quality of materials and workmanship in the store was unusual for a secular building. The reinforced concrete structure was faced externally with sandstone and internally with coloured marble from Sienna and Skyros. No expense was spared in the provision of efficient heating and lighting (including emergency lighting) installations.

'It is no coincidence that this colossal work has emerged in Düsseldorf. Here at the entrance to the huge industrial district, near the old cultural centres, it stands like a mighty focus that combines all the threads of a great modern complex . . . Just as the cathedrals of old seem all the mightier because of the adjacent houses, here too Olbrich's architecture reigns over its surroundings. The problem in the exterior form of the Warenhaus lies in the synthesis of a great number of storeys, halls and staircases to a unified whole. Here the pillar is the given factor that truly masters the bulk in an infinite series of links, but at the same time produces an extremely complex arrangement in controlling the transition from pillar to roof . . . In the Gothic cathedrals the structural mass of the pillars was resolved quite gradually into smaller finials and turrets. Here the pillars grow organically into the air . . .'

'Additionally the lay-out of the plan solution is of lucid clarity in its grouping around three light-courts in such a manner that one is continually aware of one's own position. The compact storeys, determined by the nature of the stalls, are relieved by the high light-courts. What halls are created here!'

'High marble pillars soar upwards, held by wide bands. Yellow and red flash before the eyes like the splendour of Byzantine dome-building. Above a wide coffered frieze an upper window spans lightly and ethereally. Heavy light fittings with pendants emphasise the width of the room. You can hardly get used to

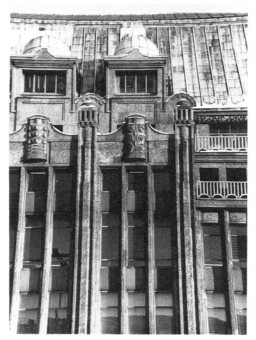

Above, left to right
Detail of main entrance, roof parapet and the carpet room.

Detail of one of the twin south gables.

using these splendid halls for prosaic sale purposes, and yet the fluctuation and mortality of earthly things might be even more overwhelming. The incomparable marble is covered with veins and the character of the material has been emphasised everywhere by inlaid bands with special ornaments.'

'The ornamental vitality of the interior is especially rich. On the wooden ramps, the floors, the doors, light fittings, radiators, and the windows there is a richness of decoration which is exemplary in spite of all the numerous new motifs. The early period of the artist appears to be favourably expressed in the maturity of the entire structure. The Düsseldorf Warenhaus unites all the gifts of the artist in a rare harmony.' (Max Creutz, 'Introduction', *Joseph M. Olbrich, Das Warenhaus Tietz in Düsseldorf,* Wasmuth, Berlin, 1909.)

Olbrich lived to see the exterior of the Warenhaus Tietz, his last and greatest building, virtually finished, and he left behind sufficient drawings and sketches of the interior for his assistant Philipp Schäfer to ensure the completion of the building almost exactly as he had intended. The Warenhaus Tietz was officially opened eight months after Olbrich's death and, although the interior has been totally altered, its external appearance remains close to the original form.

LAST DAYS

Joseph Maria Olbrich died of leukaemia on August 8th 1908 at the age of 40.

He had fallen ill shortly after the birth of his daughter, apparently just as he had taken up oil painting. Entering Düsseldorf hospital with the words 'Ich bin der Olbrich', he immediately set to work with a sketchpad, and three days later his illness was diagnosed. He was buried at Darmstadt Cemetery on August 12th. 'Modern Art has suffered a serious loss. Viennese art, one could actually say, for Olbrich was, and remained, a true Viennese artist, even in Darmstadt. He had the colourful, lively fantasy, the innate elegance and the ingratiating amiability of Schubert and Johann Strauss.' (Ludwig Hevesi, *Altkunst-Neukunst, Wien 1894-1908,* Wien, 1909, p.323.)

The loss was felt throughout Germany, but especially in Darmstadt where postcards of the funeral were available; the existence of an 'Olbrich cult' became apparent. On October 9th, 1908 a memorial service was held on the Mathildenhöhe; trumpets echoed from the top of the Wedding Tower as nine black-robed muses descended the stairs carrying golden laurel wreaths. An orchestra played excerpts from *Die Götterdämmerung.*

'Olbrich then died by chance in that year, quite suddenly, in his first full maturity, when the abuse had already been muted, for the Tower is indeed (in God's name) splendid, already a building worth seeing, and in days to come it will be the "pride" of the Hessian capital. But if only he were still alive!' (Ludwig Hevesi, *Altkunst-Neukunst, Wien 1894-1908,* Wien, 1909, p.327.)

Joseph Maria Olbrich's death in 1908 occured only ten years after the completion of his first major commission, the Secession building in Vienna. During that brief decade he had carried out a remarkable quantity and variety of work, helping to sow the seeds for the subsequent important developments in twentieth-century architecture and design.

In the early days in Vienna, the young Olbrich was taught by the established architects of the imperial capital, including some who had been involved in the historicist Ringstrasse project. His education continued during his six year period in the office of Otto Wagner. Only seven years younger than William Morris, Wagner had advocated the rejection of the retrospective styles in favour of an architecture based on function. Both Hevesi and Bahr stress how the renaissance, or 'naissance' of Viennese art at the turn of the century developed internally as a reaction against the artistic 'establishment', against the classical vocabulary of historicism it extolled, rather than from any direct foreign intervention. As a co-founder of the Vienna Secession, Olbrich helped introduce the art from abroad into the city to encourage the Austrian artists, and he assisted in the development of the characteristic 'Secessionstil' ornamentation on the pages of *Ver Sacrum.* His early work was criticised, not without some reason, by Adolf Loos, a former colleague in the Secession; the Secessionists' desire to create a total artistic environment, the 'Gesamtkunst', could stifle individual freedom and discourage further changes. Olbrich, however, always stressed the need to provide an artistic setting which could provoke an artistic response from the public.

With his radical ideas, Olbrich inevitably made many enemies in both Vienna and Darmstadt, but his work gained international respect at important exhibitions in Paris, Turin, Moscow, St. Louis and Dresden. (When Frank Lloyd Wright visited Europe in 1910 he was referred to as the 'American Olbrich'.) Olbrich was fortunate in Darmstadt to work for an enlightened patron, the Grand Duke, who saw the need for unimpeded architectural experimentation. Indeed Ernst Ludwig encouraged Olbrich to undertake commissions in his own time, just as Otto

Opposite
Warenhaus Tietz: the Great Light Court.

Joseph Maria Olbrich (22.12.1867-8.8.1908).

Sketch for a piano, probably designed for the Stifft music-room.

Pewter Wine service, c. 1901.

Wagner had allowed him to do in Vienna. On at least three occasions during his life, Olbrich made unsuccessful attempts to obtain teaching posts: in 1899 at the Vienna Kunstgewerbeschule, in 1904 at the Vienna Akademie, and in 1907 for the position of Director at the Düsseldorf Kunstgewerbeschule. In the Darmstadt Artists' Colony Olbrich was able to put the 'Gesamtkunst' principles fully into practice, devoting his energy to a wide variety of design problems, from cutlery to costume, from tapestries to posters. Olbrich's architecture of this period cannot be considered as mainstream Art Nouveau; his ornamentation was always carefully controlled and never allowed to dominate or detract from the essential practical nature of his works. His later move towards a more classical architecture, influenced by nineteenth-century Biedermeier and Italian Renaissance design, was an attempt to find a more popularly acceptable Germanic expression for his forms.

Throughout his life, Olbrich's work nevertheless retained a bold originality and inventiveness, never accepting the traditional norms without question. He designed with apparent ease and speed and his draughtsmanship was both fluent and lucid, a true reflection of his lively, exuberant character, his joy for life. Olbrich was calm and sincere, inspiring confidence in his fellow workers and pupils, though annoying his rivals on occasions. He was happily married to Claire Morawe (formerly Thum); they married in Wiesbaden in April 1903, and their daughter Marianne was born in Dresden just twenty days before Joseph Olbrich's death.

The visionary nature of Olbrich's architecture has already been mentioned; his Darmstadt projects provided inspiration for the Expressionist architects of later years, including Erich Mendelsohn, Bruno Taut and Otto Bartning. Olbrich was a founder member of the B.D.A. (Bund Deutscher Architekten) in 1903 and of the Deutscher Werkbund in October 1907 which were to play such important roles in the impending developments in architecture. Bearing in mind his last neo-classical houses, it would be difficult to speculate on the possible future direction of Olbrich's work; he would almost certainly have contributed to the important Deutscher Werkbund Exhibition of 1914 in Cologne. His memory, however, lies best in those buildings still surviving today: his Secession building in Vienna, the Wedding Tower and Colony buildings in Darmstadt and the Warenhaus Tietz in Düsseldorf.

BUILDINGS · AND · PROJECTS

1890   Project: House for Dr. D. Dimitrijević, Belgrade
1891   Project: Schlesisches Museum of Arts and Crafts, Troppau
1893   Project: Theatre, Vienna
1895   Project: Nordböhmisches Museum of Applied Arts, Reichenberg
1896   Project: 'Cobenzl-Krapfenwaldl' residential suburb, Vienna
       Project: Provincial Assembly Building, Laibach
       Project: Franzens Bridge, Vienna
1897   Project: Pavilion for the City of Vienna, Jubilee Exhibition (1898), Vienna
       Project: Art Gallery, Cracow
1897-8 Secession Building, Friedrichstrasse 12, Vienna *(altered)*
1898   1st Secession Exhibition, Horticultural Society, Vienna
       Bicycle Clubhouse, Rustenschacherallee 7, Vienna *(altered)*
       Project: Café Niedermeyer, Troppau
       Von Klarwill family grave, Döblinger Friedhof, Vienna
       Max Friedmann Villa, Hauptstrasse 27, Hinterbrühl *(altered)*
       2nd Secession Exhibition, Secession Building, Vienna
1899   4th Secession Exhibition, Secession Building, Vienna
       House for Dr. Hermann Stöhr, Kremsergasse 41, St. Pölten *(altered)*
       Interiors for Alfred Stifft, Hohe Warte 48, Vienna
       Guest room, Villa Metternich, Königswart
       Interiors for Consul Ladislaus von Dirsztay, Rennweg 25, Vienna
       Interiors for David Berl, Sühnhaus, Schottenring 7, Vienna
       Interiors for Consul Dr. Friedrich von Spitzer, Schleifmühlgasse 4, Vienna
       'Wiener Interieur', 1900 World Exposition, Paris
       Interior: Winter Exhibition of the Austrian Museum for Art and Industry (1899-1900), Vienna
       House for Hermann Bahr, Winzerstrasse 22, Wien-Ober St. Veit *(altered)*
       Reception room, 1900 World Exposition, Paris
       Project: Interiors for Weidenbusch, Frankfurt
       Interiors for Gustav Römheld, Alexandraweg 14, Darmstadt
       Project: Artist's studio, Mathildenhöhe, Darmstadt
       Ernst Ludwig Haus, Alexandraweg 26, Darmstadt *(altered)*
       Project: Watertrough, Mathildenhöhe, Darmstadt
1900   Project: Observation Tower preliminary sketches, Mathildenhöhe, Darmstadt
       Schlesinger family grave, Zentralfriedhof, Vienna
       Haus Olbrich, Alexandraweg 28, Darmstadt *(altered)*
       Haus Christiansen, Alexandraweg 24, Darmstadt *(destroyed)*
       Haus Habich, Alexandraweg 27, Darmstadt *(altered)*
       Haus Glückert I, Alexandraweg 23, Darmstadt *(altered)*
       Haus Glückert II, Alexandraweg 25, Darmstadt *(altered)*
       Haus Keller, Alexandraweg 31, Darmstadt *(altered)*
       Haus Deiters, Mathildenhöhweg 2, Darmstadt
       Glückert family grave, Alter Friedhof, Darmstadt
       House group for Wilhelm Ganss, Alexandraweg 3-5-7, Darmstadt *(altered)*
       Project: House for Dr. Eduard von Pander, Darmstadt
       Main Entrance Portal, 1901 Exhibition, Darmstadt *(destroyed)*
       Exhibition Gallery, 1901 Exhibition, Darmstadt *(destroyed)*
       Blumenhaus, 1901 Exhibition, Darmstadt *(destroyed)*
       Sales Kiosk, 1901 Exhibition, Darmstadt *(destroyed)*
       Main Restaurant, 1901 Exhibition, Darmstadt *(destroyed)*
       Fountain surround (for Habich's sculpture), Alexandraweg, Darmstadt
1901   Orchestra pavilion, 1901 Exhibition, Darmstadt *(destroyed)*
       Playhouse, 1901 Exhibition, Darmstadt *(destroyed)*
       Project: House group for Eduard Harres, Darmstadt
       Double-house for Joseph and Gustav Stade, Prinz-Christians-Weg 19-21, Darmstadt *(destroyed)*
       Project: Workers' housing, Darmstadt
1901-2 Project: Stables for Julius Glückert, Darmstadt
       House for Albert Hochstrasser, Schönberger Feld 9, Kronberg im Taunus *(altered)*
1902   House for Carl Kuntze, Halskestrasse 3, Berlin-Steglitz *(destroyed)*
       Interiors, 1902 International Exhibition, Turin
       Display for Oscar Winter, 1902 International Exhibition, Turin
       Project: Exhibition Hall for the Deutscher Steinindustrie AG, Cologne
       Project: Display for Carl Mand, 1902 Industry, Crafts and Arts Exhibition, Düsseldorf
       Project: Hotel Königswart, Königswart
       Project: Alterations to Haus Kramer, Darmstadt
       Small house for Princess Elisabeth of Hesse, Schloss Wolfsgarten
       Project: Single-family houses, Darmstadt

Project: Rosenhöhe, Darmstadt
Interiors, 1903 Exhibition of Modern Architecture, Moscow
1902-3 Music-room, Neues Palais, Darmstadt
1903 Project: House for Prof. Friedrich Sarre, Neubabelsberg
Guest-room, Hotel Clauss-Feist, Traben-Trarbach
Fountain Court and interiors, 1904 Louisiana Purchase International Exposition, St. Louis
Project: Basel Railway Station
Project: Interiors for Carlo Stratta, Turin
Music-room, 1903-4 Exhibition of the Dresdener Werkstätten für Handwerkskunst, Dresden
Three-house group, Stiftstrasse 12, Prinz-Christians-Weg 2-4, Darmstadt *(altered)*
1904 Facade for Edmund Olbrich house, Ratiborerstrasse 17, Troppau *(destroyed)*
Sculpture Studio, Ernst-Ludwig-Haus, Darmstadt
Fountain on Platanenhain, Mathildenhöhe, Darmstadt
Restaurant pavilions, 1904 Exhibition, Darmstadt *(destroyed)*
Sales Kiosks, 1904 Exhibition, Darmstadt *(destroyed)*
Project: Art Exhibition Buildings, Cologne
Project: Secession Building, Berlin
Dining-room, 1905 Exhibition of Möbelfabrik A.S. Ball, Berlin
1904-5 Project: Double-house for August Ohl, Hanau
Project: Eleonorenhotel, Darmstadt
1905 Project: House for Eduard Schwarzmann, Strassburg
Project: Swimming Pool, Darmstadt
Interiors for Waring and Gillow, London
Colour Gardens, 1905 Horticultural Exhibition, Darmstadt
Project: Factory buildings for the Deutsche Linkrustawerke Gerhard AG, Neu-Isenburg
'Der Frauen-Rosenhof' Flora Park, Cologne *(altered)*
Interiors, 3rd German Applied Arts Exhibition (1906), Dresden
Project: Garden house for Ludwig Habich, Darmstadt
Stables for Julius Glückert, Prinz-Christians-Weg 17, Darmstadt *(altered)*
1905-6 Wedding Tower and Exhibition Buildings, Mathildenhöhe, Darmstadt *(altered)*
1906 Project: Cabinet double-house, Darmstadt
Interiors, 1906 International Exhibition, Milan
Project: Opel automobile fittings
Project: Fountain colonnades, Karlsbad
House for Dr. Erwin Silber, Marbornerstrasse 9, Bad Soden bei Salmünster *(altered)*
Interiors for J. M. Pécheral, Cannes
Project: Summerhouse for Julius Glückert, Darmstadt
1906-7 Interiors, Altes Schloss, Giessen
Project: Hohler Weg Garden Suburb, Darmstadt
1906-8 Department Store for Leonhard Tietz, Königsallee, Düsseldorf *(altered)*
1907 Project: Water Towers, Hamburg
Project: Alterations to the Pariser Platz, Berlin
Project: Café Hofgarten, Darmstadt
Interiors, 1907 Cologne Exhibition
Salon and Gallery, 1907 Jubilee Exhibition, Mannheim
Luisenplatz fountains, Darmstadt
Interiors, SS 'Kronprinzessin Cecilie'
Salon, Franz Holzamer Exhibition 1907, Berlin
Worker's House for Wilhelm Opel, 1908 Hessische Exhibition, Darmstadt *(destroyed)*
Oberhessisches Haus, Olbrich-Weg 15, Darmstadt
House for Hugo Kruska (1) Pfarriusstrasse 4, Köln-Lindenthal *(destroyed)*
Project: Darmstadt Railway Station
1908 House for Max Clarenbach, Duisburger strasse 15a, Wittlaer bei Düsseldorf *(altered)*
Court President's Office, Justice Hall, Mainz
Interiors for Julius Glückert, Alexandraweg 23, Darmstadt
Garden for Julius Glückert, Alexandraweg 25, Darmstadt
House for Hugo Kruska (II) (van Geleen), Pfarriusstrasse 6, Köln-Linderthal *(destroyed)*
House for Joseph Feinhals, Lindenallee 5, Köln-Marienburg *(destroyed)*
House for Walter Banzhaf, Am Südpark 15, Köln-Marienburg *(destroyed)*
Shop for Theodor Althoff, Hochstrasse 23, Gladbeck *(destroyed)*
Project: Shop for Theodor Althoff, Recklinghausen

BIBLIOGRAPHY

BOOKS:
Hermann Bahr, *Secession,* Wiener Verlag, Vienna, 1900.
Max Creutz, *Das Warenhaus Tietz in Düsseldorf,* Berlin, 1909.
Ludwig Hevesi, *Acht Jahre Secession 1897-1905,* Vienna, 1906.
Ludwig Hevesi, *Altkunst-Neukunst, Wien 1894-1908,* Vienna, 1909.
Joseph A. Lux, *Joseph Maria Olbrich,* Wasmuth, Berlin, 1919.
Architektur von Olbrich I-III, Wasmuth, Berlin, 1901-1914.
Ideen von Olbrich, Gerlach & Schenk, Vienna, 1900; Leipzig, 1904.
The Open University, *History of Architecture and Design 1890-1939,* units 3-4, 9-10,
    Milton Keynes, 1975.
Nicholas Powell, *The Arts in Vienna 1898-1908,* London, 1974.
Robert Schmutzler, *Jugendstil,* Stuttgart, 1962.
Karl H. Schreyl, *Joseph Maria Olbrich: Die Zeichnungen in der Kunstbibliothek,* Berlin, 1972.
Peter Vergo, *Art in Vienna 1898-1918,* London, 1975.
Giulia Veronesi, *Joseph Maria Olbrich,* Milan, 1948.

ARTICLES:
(Several contributions unless noted)
Architectural Design, 37, 1967, p.566. Robert Judson Clark, 'J. M. Olbrich 1867-1908'.
Der Architekt
L'Architettura, May-September 1970.
Darmstädter Tagblatt
Darmstädter Zeitung
Dekorative Kunst
Deutsche Bauzeitung
Deutsche Kunst und Dekoration
Hohe Warte
Innendekoration
Das Interieur
Kunst im Hessen und am Mittelrhein, 7, 1967. R. J. Clark, 'Olbrich and Vienna';
    H. C. Hoffmann, 'Joseph M. Olbrichs architektonische Werk für die Ausstellung "Ein
    Dokument Deutscher Kunst" auf der Mathildenhöhe zu Darmstadt 1901'.
Schweizerische Bauzeitung
The Studio
Studio International, April 1971, pp.168-9. Peter Hauptmann, 'The house of the Vienna
    Secession Movement'.
The Studio Special Summer Number, 1906. A. S. Levetus, 'Modern Decorative Art in Austria';
    Hugo Haberfeld, 'The Architectural Revival in Austria'.
Ver Sacrum (1898-1903)
Werk, 4, 1966, pp.71-3. Othmar Birkner, 'Joseph Maria Olbrich'.
Werk, 5, 1966, pp.105-7. Othmar Birkner, 'Das Warenhaus Tietz in Düsseldorf von
    Joseph Maria Olbrich'.
Die Zeit, 14.8.1908, Otto Wagner, 'Josef Olbrich', p.l.

CATALOGUES:
Ein Dokument Deutscher Kunst 1901, Hauptkatalog, Munich, 1901.
Grossherzog Ernst Ludwig und die Ausstellung der Künstler-Kolonie in Darmstadt, Koch,
    Darmstadt, 1901.
Ausstellung der Künstler-Kolonie, Darmstadt, 1904.
Illustrierte Katalog der Hessischen Landesausstellung für freie und angewandte Kunst,
    Darmstadt, 1908.
Olbrich-Ausstellung Kunstgewerbe-Museum, Düsseldorf, 1908.
Olbrich-Gedächtnis-Ausstellung Ernst Ludwig Haus, Darmstadt, October, 1908.
Joseph Maria Olbrich Ausstellung, Akademie der Künste, Berlin, Munich, 1910.
J. Olbrich-Zeichnungen, Berlin, 1912.
Joseph Maria Olbrich 1867-1908, Das Werk des Architekten, Darmstadt, Vienna, Berlin, 1967.
Ein Dokument Deutscher Kunst 1901-1976, Darmstadt, 1976.

THE MATHILDENHÖHE, DARMSTADT

Key

1 ERNST LUDWIG HAUS (1899)
2 HAUS OLBRICH (1900)
3 HAUS CHRISTIANSEN (1900)
4 HAUS GLÜCKERT I (1900)
5 HAUS GLÜCKERT II (1900)
6 HAUS HABICH (1900)
7 HAUS KELLER (1900)
8 HAUS DEITERS (1900)
9 EXHIBITION GALLERY (1901 EXHIBITION)
10 HAUS BEHRENS (1901) — ARCHITECT: PETER BEHRENS
11 RUSSIAN CHAPEL (1898) — ARCHITECT: BENOIS
12 WEDDING TOWER (1905-6)
13 EXHIBITION BUILDINGS (1905-6)
14 OBERHESSISCHES HAUS (1907)
15 ENTRANCE PORTAL (1901 EXHIBITION)
16 POSTCARD KIOSK (1901 EXHIBITION)
17 CATALOGUE KIOSK (1901 EXHIBITION)
18 RESTAURANT (1901 EXHIBITION)
19 BLUMENHAUS (1901 EXHIBITION)
20 SPIELHAUS (1901 EXHIBITION)
21 ORCHESTRA PAVILION (1901 EXHIBITION)

All buildings were designed by Joseph Olbrich except where noted. Extant buildings by Olbrich are indicated in solid black.

ACKNOWLEDGEMENTS

Thanks go to the following institutions and individuals for making material available for publication: Berlin Kunstbibliothek (Staatliche Museen Preussischer Kulturbesitz: photographer K. H. Paulmann) — 11 (top and bottom); 21, 26 (bottom), 41 (right), 46 (right), 50, 57 (top), 97 (top left and right), 104 (both), 116 (left), 129 (top left and right), 130 (middle), 134 (bottom), 139 (top), 148 (right), in addition to providing photographs from which illustrations have been redrawn; Tim Benton — frontispiece, 72 (bottom left), 91 (top right); University of Glasgow (Mackintosh collection) — 138 (bottom); Ezio Godoli — 12 (right), 71; Hessisches Landesmuseum, Darmstadt — 99, 147, 148 (left); Ian Latham — 54 (top), 58 (right), 70, 72 (top and bottom right), 81 (both), 91 (left), 105, 106 (both), 107 (both), 108, 130 (top), 145 (top, middle and below); Giorgio Pezzato — 19; Frank Russell — 54 (bottom left and right); Vienna Secession (Vereinigung Bildender Künstler Wiener Secession: photographer Helmut Kedro) — 22, 23 (top, middle and bottom right), 24 (right), 25 (left and right), 27 (bottom), 28 (top and bottom), 29 (top and bottom), 30 (top and bottom), 31 (left and right), 32 (left), 33 (bottom left); Museum der Stadt Wien — 12 (left).

All other illustrations are from the following contemporary sources: Architektur von Olbrich I-III, Wasmuth, Berlin, 1901-1914; *Ideen von Olbrich,* Gerlach & Schenk, Vienna, 1900 and Leipzig, 1904; *Deutsche Kunst und Dekoration; Meister der Innenkunst: Haus eines Kunstfreundes von M. H. Baillie Scott,* A. Koch, Darmstadt, 1902; *The Studio; Ver Sacrum.*

INDEX

Figures in italics refer to pages containing illustrations only.

Abels, Ludwig   35
Aloys, Ludwig   10
Alt, Rudolf von   14
Altes Schloss, Giessen   126; *121, 127*
American Institute of Architects   129
Ashbee, C. R.   48

Bacher, Rudolf   14
Bahr, Haus, Ober St. Veit   46-47
Bahr, Hermann   13, 17, 46-47, 52, 94, 147
Baillie Scott, M. H.   48, 58, 138
Banzhaf, Villa, Cologne   135; *136*
Bartel, August   9, 10
Bartning, Otto   148
Basel Station Competition   132-133
Bauer, Leopold   10, 32
'Beaulieu' (Haus Keller)   86
Behrens, Haus   94
Behrens, Peter   49, 50, 52, 94, 98, 126, 130
Benois   50
Berl, Apartment for David   35; *37*
Berl, David   35
Biedermeier   126, 148
Billing, Hermann   130
'Blaue Haus'   98; *99*
'Blumenhaus', 1901   94; *95*
Böhm, Adolf   16, 32, 42
Bonatz, Martin and Taut   134
Bosselt, Haus   78
Bosselt, Rudolf   49, 50, 52, 70, 78, 98; *54*
Bramante   135
Brantzky, Franz   130
Brurein   134
Bund Deutscher Architekten   148
Bürck, Paul   49, 50, 52, 92, 93, 98
Burne-Jones, Edward   14

Christiansen, Hans   49, 50, 52, 68-69, 93, 96, 98
Christiansen, Haus   68-69
Cissarz, Johann Vincenz   98
Clarenbach, House for Max   134-135
Cologne Exhibition, 1906   130
Concert Pavilion, 1904   98
Crane, Walter   14, 17, 32
Cycling Club, Pavilion for Vienna State and
   Court Officials   34

Darmstadt Artists' Colony   48-119, 148
   1901 Exhibition   50-97, 98, 138
   1904 Exhibition   98-99, 120
   1908 Exhibition   116, 118, 138
'Darmstädter Zimmer', Paris, 1900   49
Darmstadt Station Competition   133-134
Deininger, Julius   9, 13
Deiters, Haus   90-91
Deiters, Wilhelm   90
Deutsche Kunst und Dekoration   49, 78, 127
Deutscher Tapetenzeitung   49
Deutscher Werkbund   148
Diehl, J. W.   92, 93
Dimitrijewic, House for Dr G.   9
Doczi, Ludwig von   34
'Dreihäusergruppe'   98-99, 120
Drexler brothers   10

Ebhardt, Bodo von   130
'Eckhaus' ('Holzgiebelhaus')   99
'Ein Dokument Deutscher Kunst', 1901
   50-97, 98, 138
'Ein kleines Haus'   46
Eleonorenhotel, Darmstadt   130
Elisabeth, Princess of Hesse   126

Engelhart, Josef   13
Engler, Otto   143
Engler, Paul   143
Ernst Ludwig, Grand Duke of Hesse   48, 50,
   100, 126, 138, 147
Ernst Ludwig Haus   52-57, 98
Exhibition Buildings, Darmstadt   100-111

Feinhals, House for Joseph   135; *137*
Felix, Eugen   13
Fischer, Felix   34-35
Fischer, Theodor   130
Fischl, Carl   10
Franz Joseph I   13, 17
Franz Joseph I, Jubilee Memorial Church   34
'Frauenrosenhof', Cologne   130
Fremdenblatt   34
Friedmann, Villa   42-45, 52; *14*
Friedrichstrasse, Secession Building site
   24-33

Gallery (Gebäude für Fläschenkunst), 1901
   93; *94, 95*
Ganss, House group for Wilhelm   120
Gartenbaugesellschaft, Vienna   17
Gartenvorstadt, Hohlen Weg   138
Geleen, House for Frau van   135; *136*
Glasgow Four   16
Glückert Haus, Grosses   70-77, 78, 118-119;
   frontispiece, 6
   1908 Redecorations   70, 118-119
Glückert Haus, Kleines   70, 78-81; *72*
Glückert, Julius   70, 78, 118, 126
Glückert stables   *82-83*
Grand Duke of Hesse (see Ernst Ludwig)
Grasset, Eugène   14
Greiner, Daniel   98, 99

Habich, Haus   78, 84-85; *51*
Habich, Ludwig   49, 50, 52, 84, 98, 99; *62*
Hall of Honour, Academy Project   12
Hamburg, Water Towers   130; *132*
Harres Häusergruppe   120; *121*
'Haus eines Kunstfreundes', 1901   138
Haustein, Paul   98
Henneberg, Hugo   37
Hevesi, Ludwig   8, 9, 25, 31, 42, 47, 58, 147
Hietzing, Vienna   48
Hochstrasser, House for Albert   120, 129,
   138
Hochzeitsturm (see Wedding Tower)
Hoffmann, Josef   10, 12, 13, 14, 16, 17, 32,
   37, 48
Hoffmann, K.   50
Hoffmann, Ludwig   126
Hofpavillon, Schönbrunn   10; *12*
Hohe Warte, Vienna   34, 37, 48
Huber, Patriz   49, 50, 52, 69, 81, 84, 98

Kaan, Artur   34
Kainradl, Leo   13
Karlskirche, Vienna   26
Karlsplatz Station, Vienna   10; *12*
Karpellus, Adolf   13
Kedl, Rudolf   26
Keller, Haus   86-89
Kiosks, Postcard and Catalogue, 1901   93
Klarwill family grave   34
'Kleinwohnungskolonie'   112, 138
Klimt, Georg   26
Klimt, Gustav   13, 14, 18, 29, 47; *17*
Klinger, Max   14
Klingholz, Professor   134

Kment, Hubert   9
Knopff, Ferdinand   14, 17
Koch, Alexander   49, 126
Königswart Hotel Project   129, 138
Kotera, Jan   32
Krämer, Johann Viktor   14
Krauss   32
Kreis, Wilhelm   143
Kruska, House for Hugo   135; *136*
Künstlerhaus, Vienna   13, 14
Kuntze, Villa for Carl   125; *122*
Kurzweil, Max   13

Le Corbusier   84
Lichtwark, Alfred   58
Liebermann, Max   14
Loos, Adolf   84, 147
Low Cost Housing Projects   138-140
Lueger, Karl   21
Luisenplatz, Darmstadt   132; *133*
Luntz, Viktor   34

Mackintosh, Charles Rennie   *138*
Mahler, Gustav   37
Mannheim Exhibition, 1907   130, 132; *133*
Mathildenhöhe, Darmstadt   50
Mautner family   24
Mayreder, Julius   14
Mayreder, Rudolf   21
Mendelsohn, Erich   93, 148
Metternich, Villa   129
Moll, Carl   13, 14, 24, 37
Morawe, Claire   148
Morris, William   32, 48, 147
Moser, Koloman   13, 14, 16, 26, 32, 37; *31*
Mucha, Alphonse   14, 17
Muthesius, Hermann   127

Neue Palais, Darmstadt   48, 126
Niedermeyer, Café   40, 130; *20, 41*

Oberhessisches Haus   116-117, 135
Ohmann, Friedrich   12
Olbrich, Edmund   9
Olbrich, Haus   58-67, 81; *front cover,*
   half-title
Olbrich, House for Edmund   130; *131*
Opel, Wilhelm   112
Opel Worker's House   112-115, 138
Orchestra Pavilion, 1901   96

Pankok, Bernhard   130
Pantheon (Ruhmeshalle) project   10
Paris, 1900 Exhibition   32, 37, 49; *38-39*
Peruzzi   135
Playhouse for Elisabeth von Hessen   126
Plecnik, Josef   32
Poelzig, Hans   94, 130
Porzellanschlösschen, Darmstadt   49
'Predigerhaus' (Graue Haus)   98; *99*
Provisional Buildings, 1901 Exhibition   92-97
Pützer, Professor   134

Ramspek, Lise   126
Ratzel, Friedrich   130
Rehberg and Lipp   143
Reichenberg Museum   12
Restaurant Pavilion, 1901   93
Restaurant Pavilion, 1904   98
Ringstrasse, Vienna   9, 13, 147
Rodin, August   14, 17
Roller, Alfred   32
Rome Prize   10, 12; *11*

Römheld, Gustav   120
Russian Chapel, Darmstadt   50, 92

St. Louis Exhibition, 1904   127-128
Sarre, House for Friedrich   126
Schäfer, Philipp   145
Schimkowitz, Othmar   26; *32*
Schöne, Ludwig   42
Schreider, Carl   31
Schumacher, Fritz   58
Secession, Vienna   13-33, 34, 48
   Secession Building   18-33, 34, 148
   1st Exhibition   17, 24
   2nd Exhibition   32; *33*
   4th Exhibition   47; *33*
Seidl, Karl   13
Siccardsburg, August Siccard von   13
'Siebenerklub'   13, 16
Silber, Haus   141-142
Sitte, Camillo   9
'Sommersitz eines Kunstfreundes'   127
Sperl, Café   13
'Spielhaus', 1901   94-96; *97*
Spitzer, Dr. Friedrich   37
'Staatsgefängnis' (State prison)   34; *15*
Stade, Doppelhaus   120; *121*
Stadtbahn, Vienna   10
Stifft, House for Alfred   34; *36, 148*
Stix, Carl   96
Stöhr, Ernst   14, 34
Stöhr, House and shop for Dr. Hermann   34;
   20
Storck, Karl   130
Strasser, Artur   32; *33*
Stratta, Carlo   127; *128*
Strauss, Richard   96
Stuck, Franz   14
Studio, The   13, 16, 17, 69, 126
Swoboda, Eduard   12

Taut, Bruno   94, 134, 148
Theatre project   10; *11*
Theatre Studio, 1901   96; *97*
Tietz, Warenhaus   135, 143-146, 148
Tiffany, Louis Comfort   93
Turin Exhibition, 1902   49, 116, 126

Uhde, Fritz von   14
Urban, Joseph   13

Ver Sacrum   14, 15-16, 52, 147
Vetterlein, Dr.   130
Victoria, Queen of England   48
Vienna Secession   13-33, 34, 147
Voysey, C. F. A.   25

Wagner, Otto   10, 12, 13, 14, 34, 147
   Academy of Fine Arts   12, 32
   Linke Wienzeile 38   40; *12*
   Postsparkasse   12
   Steinhof Church   12
Walton, E. A.   14
Warenhaus Tietz   135, 143-146, 148
Wedding Tower (Hochzeitsturm)   93,
   100-111, 147, 148
Whistler, James   17
'Wiener Zimmer', Paris, 1900   37; *38-39*
Wittgenstein family   24
Wolfsgarten bei Langen   126
Wright, Frank Lloyd   129, 147

'Zum Blauen Freihaus'   13